Endoi

"In *The Hero in Heroin* Mindy's story conveys an alternative experience of reality and human consciousness vital to how some view the soul, spirit, and the potential non-physical realms of being. Mindy is an engaging storyteller and has masterfully depicted the potential for one special human being's spiritual transformation. The synthesis, synchronicities, and balancing of Mindy and Micah's experiences exemplify the evolutionary nature of unconditional Love."

Dr. John Demartini
Best-selling author of *Inspired Destiny*

This absorbing and brave book reveals sorrow and hope, walking hand in hand, bound together by compassion. With great storytelling skills, Mindy reveals the emergence of unconditional love as she strives to support her son and his addiction. Micah's own writings about his challenges bring greater depth to a book essential to those who find themselves in similar situations.

Christine Page, MD
Author of the *Healing Power of the Sacred Woman*

Moving, graceful, and poetic. Challenging, tragic, and transforming. Inspiring, frightening, and empowering. Rarely has a book touched me so deeply. From drugs to destiny, from sorrow to synchronicity, we are invited to enter Mindy and Micah's minds and hearts, and through this extraordinary journey, awaken. Be prepared for your current vision of life and love to be enriched and elevated.

Gary E. Schwartz, PhD
Professor of Psychology, Medicine, Neurology,
Psychiatry, and Surgery at the University of Arizona
Author of *The Afterlife Experiments and The Sacred Promise*

THE HEROIN HEROIN

A Mother and Son's Journey on Both Sides of the Veil

MINDY MIRALIA

BALBOA.
PRESS

A DIVISION OF HAY HOUSE

Balboa Press books may be ordered through booksellers or by contacting:

Balboa Press
A Division of Hay House
1663 Liberty Drive
Bloomington, IN 47403
www.balboapress.com
1 (877) 407-4847

Because of the dynamic nature of the Internet, any web addresses or links contained in this book may have changed since publication and may no longer be valid. The views expressed in this work are solely those of the author and do not necessarily reflect the views of the publisher, and the publisher hereby disclaims any responsibility for them.

The author of this book does not dispense medical advice or prescribe the use of any technique as a form of treatment for physical, emotional, or medical problems without the advice of a physician, either directly or indirectly. The intent of the author is only to offer information of a general nature to help you in your quest for emotional and spiritual well-being. In the event you use any of the information in this book for yourself, which is your constitutional right, the author and the publisher assume no responsibility for your actions.

Any people depicted in stock imagery provided by Thinkstock are models, and such images are being used for illustrative purposes only.
Certain stock imagery © Thinkstock.

Print information available on the last page.

ISBN: 978-1-5043-2637-7 (sc)
ISBN: 978-1-5043-2639-1 (hc)
ISBN: 978-1-5043-2638-4 (e)

Library of Congress Control Number: 2015900324

Balboa Press rev. date: 03/03/2015

Our battered suitcases were piled on the sidewalk again;
we had longer ways to go. But no matter, the road is life.
~ Jack Kerouac, *On the Road*

In honor of the life and talents of Micah Aaron Matthew Felcman.

To Micah's beloved children:
May you know and feel your father's love for you
through these stories and writings.

To all mothers (and fathers) on Earth who have lost a child:
Our hearts have touched and shared deep pain. Now my
wish is to share with you eternal hope and love.

To all families who have a loved one struggling with addiction or illness:
May you have greater understanding and awareness to find peace.

To any fellow human dealing with addiction:
No matter how minor or severe the addiction, know you have
purpose and are loved beyond measure! May you realize your
innate power and inner strength.

Contents

Preface xiii

Acknowledgments xv

Introduction xvii

Part One
The Journey Begins

1   Miracle Baby 3
2   Lubbock 8
3   Past Meets Present 10
4   The Hero Arrives 13
5   What's in a Name? 15
6   Bound for Foreign Lands 17
7   Surprises in Singapore 21
8   Back in Houston: A Boy's Cry for his Father 27
9   Boulder: Landlocked 32
10 Dubai: A Perfect Life 36
11 First Losses 41
12 The Drawings 45
13 Mauritius: Stranded 49
14 Goa: Riots 52
15 Back in Dubai: Seeds of War 56
16 Baton Rouge: Politics, Religion, and Poetry 60
17 Southern California: Earthquakes 67
18 Charlotte: Something Major Changes 72
19 Get Thee Behind Me, Satan! 76

20 The Warning...79

21 Tough Love...84

22 Energy Medicine...87

23 The Truth about Michael..................................90

24 Heroin...95

25 The Road to Recovery—Again..............................97

26 Affirming Life..100

27 Across the Generations....................................102

28 Michael Leaves for the Last Time.........................107

29 The Circle of Life..109

30 Heartbreak..112

31 Hope..115

32 Death's-Door Choice.......................................117

33 March 29, 2011..121

34 Accepting Death...129

Part Two

The Healing: The Hero Returns

35 The Bead..135

36 Sinclaire's Call..138

37 The Swing...140

38 Micah Pays a Visit..143

39 The Pocket Watch..148

40 Thank You...152

41 The Help..153

42 Kitchen Conversation......................................157

43 Robin Tekwelus Youngblood.................................160

44 T-Shirt Quilts..169

45 Full-Court Press..172

46 12-12-12..179

47 The Best Christmas Ever...................................184

48 John of God...186

49 The Agreement...191

Part Three
The Hero's Innermost Cave: Writings of
Micah Aaron Matthew Felcman

Untitled (age 11)..197
Stay or Go (Age 12) 198
Hugs (Age 13) 199
Costumed Couples 200
A Brief Introduction..204
Outcast...209
The First Buzz...211
Evil Seeds..214
Let Us Dance 220
Consequences...222
I'm Sorry, Daughter..227
My Children 229
Because of You...230
Fear and Loathing in Oahu 233
Here We Go Again 235
It's Been Years Since My Last Confession 237
Precious Medical Moments 239
June 22, 2009..241
Afraid...244
Envious!...246
Stuck in This Realm 248
Monkeys 251
Today...253

Afterword 261
About the Author...263

Preface

There still exists in humanity a primitive fear of the dark and of death that limits our comprehension of love and wisdom. We are here on earth to develop our understanding of these elements of growth and the inherent powers within them. By acknowledging them, we learn how to eliminate our fears and use these powers to experience and work toward unconditional love in the physical realm.

Through the journey of addiction with my son, Micah Aaron Matthew Felcman, I was forced to deal with much darkness and, ultimately, death. But I also learned a great deal about healing: I learned that whatever is lost will be replaced by that which is greater, stronger, and more beneficial to all humans. I learned the truth of the infinite potential within each human. I learned the extremes of duality: form-formless, light–dark, good-bad, black–white, love-hate,—and that each has purpose in God's creation. I learned that with God, *all* things are possible, not *some* things.

Once we are willing to balance the two extremes, we no longer need the pain and suffering of addiction or any other illness to move us from our innate homeostasis and God-given state of equilibrium. We truly have a choice to evolve and experience a higher, more aware perspective.

It is my passion to serve as a catalyst, communicator, and facilitator—and to give back in service to others all that I have learned and experienced in order to help others discover this new balance. The greatest legacies I can leave my family, loved ones, and humanity are spiritual ones: unwavering trust in God's love and wisdom, steadfast endurance, courage, patience, and hope; the knowledge (the remembering) of the perfect peace that is within us prior to our birth; and the awakening of the potency and power of the spiritual (the formless, the invisible) over the material (the form, the visible).

The healing messages of this book are for humankind, independent of race, religion, culture, or beliefs.

I believe that when we understand why addiction or illness is present in our lives, it becomes possible for us to know and live in peace, harmony, and optimal health. To this end, I have written *The Hero in Heroin,* in the hope that it will bring light to the invisible epidemic occurring in this country and to provide a new paradigm for healing.

Acknowledgments

It is with heartfelt gratitude that I thank Reverend Chris Andrews for his loving support and guidance at a time in my life where mysterious and mystical events occurred with me daily. His acceptance of me allowed a safe place for my gifts to emerge, and I am forever grateful that he realized this.

I thank all the teachers who have graciously challenged me to grow. You opened the door, and I stepped in. You walked before me, yet you allowed me to find my way.

To my family and friends who love me and have supported me unconditionally during the most difficult times of my life: I could not have made the journey without you.

I thank Jennifer Read Hawthorne for her brilliant editing skills, patience, and ability to help me bring clarity to my thoughts and messages.

To my invisibles—guides, angels, masters, deceased loved ones, and others in spirit—without your love and wisdom, this book would not have been written. Thank you for embarking on this creative journey with me. It has been a true partnership.

I am especially grateful for my husband and partner, Rock, who has loved, nurtured, and encouraged me from the beginning. Thank you for being by my side.

Introduction

The archetype of the hero described by Joseph Campbell in his classic work *The Hero's Journey* is an individual who embarks on a journey of initiation and then discovers an inner knowledge or greater spiritual power—the treasure within. Along the way, he encounters many threats to his survival that compromise his journey to empowerment—challenges and forces that he must overcome.

But as the hero faces these obstacles, his true Self emerges. Eventually, he returns home bearing some element of the treasure he has discovered, which has the power to transform the world as the hero himself has been transformed.

My son, Micah, lived such a hero's journey. In this book, I share this journey—our lives together in physical form from his, the Hero's, birth to his death (part 1), our continued journey—the Hero's return with messages and lessons for all (part 2), and finally, his writings—insight into the Hero's innermost thoughts while incarnate (part 3).

The following sections describe what you'll find in this book. Please note that some names have been changed to protect the privacy of people whose lives touched ours during this journey.

Part One: The Journey Begins

Micah Felcman was not supposed to have been born. In part 1, I share the story of his birth and the years of his life when our family lived and traveled around the globe as Micah's father and I both worked internationally. Micah and his brother constantly tried to put down roots as we moved from place to place. Micah was a deeply spiritual child, enriched by his early life journeys. But at the age of fifteen, he was caught by the allure of drugs. His "first buzz" was from marijuana, behind the theater where he was supposed to be watching a movie. Then, over the next sixteen years, he experimented with cocaine, every prescription medication he could get his hands on, and ultimately, heroin—the only drug he said he could not stop when *he* wanted.

The life of a heroin addict is a desperate one. Like any other, heroin addiction destroys the user and his or her family. In the case of my son, despite the endless cycles of relapse and recovery, the misery caused by his heroin dependency caused him to take his own life at the age of thirty-one.

I have asked myself a thousand times whether I could have avoided this tragedy by doing anything differently in raising Micah. I don't know the answer, and sadly, Micah's father couldn't help me. The stress of constantly being uprooted and forced to move all over the globe was hard enough on Micah, and Micah's father was largely absent—both physically as well as emotionally—the cause of which we would learn much too late.

During his life, I did everything humanly possible to help him overcome addiction. I loved Micah dearly, and before drugs came between us, we were very close. But once I had the courage to look at myself and understand my role in his disease, I shifted from my own unhealthy family dynamic of co-dependency to a consciousness I had not previously known. I studied everything available about new ways of healing: energy medicine, quantum physics, thought, consciousness, the biology of belief, even the impact of our environment. You name it, I studied it. Had it not been for my son and the impact of his lessons of addiction, I would not have become the person I am today.

But countless visits to counselors, psychologists, psychiatrists, and 12-Step meetings and programs did not seem to quite get there for Micah or me. So the helplessness I felt at his death was beyond comprehension, because something inside me knew there was more.

Part 2: The Healing—The Hero Returns

I was right. Micah's death was not the end of our journey together. Within weeks of his passing, signs and messages began to appear letting me know that my son was trying to communicate with me. Micah had died angry, and that anger continued on the other side until he was able to heal and purify those parts of himself.

My spiritual gifts and "vision" of things unseen had been developing for many years by the time Micah died—but to have my son drop objects in front of me or show up in my kitchen in subtle form from the other side of the veil was almost more than I could handle at times!

It also soon became clear that Micah had left for a reason—and was now returning for a reason. It seems he was catapulted into the next version of himself after experiencing the isolation in this lifetime caused by drugs—his call to the "adventure" of heroin had made his life on earth impossible to continue as it was. But he returned from the other side to show me the workings of the invisible world and its impact on addiction, specifically the heroin addiction rampant in our society today.

The stories that I share in part 2 validate to me the "work," healing, and purification of his soul that Micah did on the other side of the veil—all the while keeping me in the loop and helping me to heal and learn also. His work on the other side—and the work we did together after he crossed over—show how powerful the spirit world is and how important it is for society to reconnect with the spiritual aspects of the human condition. He was specific about the responsibility of the soul and the impacts of "spirit attachments"—lifetime to lifetime.

It seems Micah did indeed have "treasure" to bring home. In December 2012, he returned once again in spirit—this time restored and redeemed. It felt as if he were letting his loved ones know he was moving on, and in some ways, he was saying good-bye for now. He wanted to make certain I knew and understood he was truly Home. He needed me to be at peace and to live the remainder of my earthly life in joy, knowing that the healing I had so desperately desired to impart to him had occurred.

Together, Micah and I achieved our divine mission in this lifetime and healed the lineage of addiction that had plagued our family lines interdimensionally and multigenerationally—far beyond the time-space our brains can conceive of.

Part 3: The Hero's Innermost Cave: Writings of Micah Aaron Matthew Felcman

Micah was a prolific writer who was not afraid to commit his innermost thoughts to paper. His writings reveal the mind of a sometimes conflicted, sometimes tortured, but always deeply spiritual human being. From the poems he wrote as a child to the prose and poetry of his later years, his writing is compelling and relevant.

I had no idea, however, just how prolific Micah was until about a year after his death, when I got a phone call from the mother of the woman he had married in 2008. When Micah had a really bad relapse in early 2009, Micah's wife's mother drove to Maine to move her daughter home. It was there that she noticed a box on the floor in the basement. She opened it and saw all of Micah's journals and a few pictures. She grabbed the box, feeling someday he would want to have it—and she had kept it safe until the day in April 2012 when I got her call.

Within the week, my husband and I drove to meet her in western North Carolina. Afterward, the box stayed in the trunk of my car for a long time. Then I moved it to the file cabinet in my office, where it sat for another month. Finally, I opened it. I was floored to find many of Micah's handwritten journals, along with writings done on an old Underwood typewriter, some of the letters of which had made holes in the paper. I was overwhelmed, and I didn't know what to do.

I have since started putting Micah's work on my computer, with the intention of publishing it in the future. In the meantime, part 3 introduces you to my son through some selected writings of his—giving you a very different perspective on the story told from my point of view in parts 1 and 2!

In these writings you will find his expression of spirit attachments and thought forms, and references to past lives as a Roman, Asian, and Native American. Though he lived with the darkness of the "monkey" of addiction, he was never far from the same teaching or learning I received in my quest for light and healing. He was a dark messenger of light.

★ ★ ★

In recent human history, we have experienced the Industrial Revolution, a technological revolution—and now a spiritual consciousness revolution that calls us to be present, raise our awareness, and expand our capacity to learn how we can alleviate much of our own pain and suffering.

While there are many causes of addiction, Micah's message to humanity is a spiritual one. Please accept this treasure and open yourselves to the deep healing that can occur when you embrace the invisible.

It gives me a deep comforting sense that "things seen
are temporal and things unseen are eternal."
~ Helen Keller

PART ONE

The Journey Begins

1

Miracle Baby

Michael and I met in an immunology class at the University of Houston in late 1976. I noticed him on Day One because he was "older," wore a roadster cap, and had on a forest-green V-neck sweater with the initials MWF scrawled in white across the upper left side. No one else in the class was dressed in this preppy, distinctive, older-person manner—and it really made him stand out.

He was a handsome man—physically fit with bluish eyes, beautiful piano- keyboard teeth, and a thick mustache. Some said he resembled Tom Selleck, and he did. He sat at the front of the classroom, the good student often first to answer the professor's questions—while I sat at the back of the room dissecting him. Laughing to my work colleague Kelly, who sat to my left, I girlishly giggled loudly enough for others to hear, "That guy has to wear a sweater to remind him which days to come to class: Monday-Wednesday-Friday!"

Eventually I met this MWF guy with the roadster cap who was eight years my senior, and we started dating. Over the next weeks and months, we had a lot of fun together—we even became highly competitive in our pre-med studies.

Then, in the summer of 1978, Michael decided to attend Texas Tech, and he moved to Lubbock. I was in my last year of undergraduate school, with twenty-one hours left to complete, so it wasn't feasible for me to consider joining him. We had professed our love for one another, but admittedly, I felt somewhat confused by his sudden departure.

Nonetheless, I believed if things between us were to work out, they would, and if not, they wouldn't. I worked at the University of Texas Medical School in the physiology department, so between my work and my studies, I barely had time to eat—let alone spend much time pondering romance. I had a long road ahead of me, and I was doing everything possible to position myself for the future by getting as much hands-on experience as I could and getting to know the players in the medical school. I knew these things would give me an advantage when it came time for me to apply.

The new school semester began, and although I missed Michael, my life went on. Everything seemed to be falling into a regular routine when, three weeks into the semester, I noticed how difficult it was for me to walk the three city blocks between my car and my classrooms—and even the short distance from one class to another. I felt winded, as if I'd run a 100-yard dash at breakneck speed. I had no energy and basically felt sick, all over, all the time. I'd drive from school to work and somehow make it through the remainder of each day, only to go home and have to study, do homework, and make dinner—then crash and start all over again the next morning.

This "illness" continued for weeks. I had been the picture of health, active and vivacious, and now I had contracted what seemed like a terrible virus of some kind. I felt worried, so in early October, I made an appointment with my favorite doctor, Dale Brown, to find out what in the world could possibly be wrong with me. My mother met me at his office.

Dr. Brown examined me. He asked questions, drew blood, and took a urine sample. Thirty minutes later, his nurse escorted me to his office, where I sat and waited. His office was filled with photos—on the wall, the shelves, and his desk. I was snooping at handwritten notes on his desk when I heard the door open behind me. He gently touched my right shoulder as he passed by.

He sat down in the chair, put his feet on the desk, and leaned back. Locking his hands behind his head and looking me squarely in the eyes, he said, "Min, what do you think is wrong with you?"

"I don't know. That's why I'm here. Do I have a virus?" I asked.

He took his feet off the desk and leaned his body and face into my space. Again he asked, "Now, Min, WHAT do you think is wrong with you?"

I had never seen him act this way before, and I was somewhat dumbfounded. I looked around the room at all those pictures. My mind raced. I scanned his face and then looked at the statues on his desk. "Am I pregnant?" I asked.

"Yes, yes you are," he said, somewhat seriously, acting differently from the way he had every other time I had been around him.

"HOW DID THAT HAPPEN?" I blurted out. "You told me I couldn't have children—and that if I ever wanted to try, I would have to really work at it, using fertility drugs and God only knows what else!"

Silence filled the room. Fractions of seconds seemed to turn into hours, and I felt as if I were in a time abyss. The silence got deeper and vaster, and I felt completely blank—a feeling I had never experienced before.

The silence was broken when he asked, "What do you want to do?"

He knew I wasn't married. He also knew that he, along with an internist and an endocrinologist, had sat me down years before—when I was in early adolescence—and explained that I had a condition that made my chances of having a child slim to none.

Suddenly, I snapped out of the blankness, and with sheer joy, great surprise, and pure delight, I said, "What do you mean? I want to keep it!" At those words, his body relaxed, and he became the person I had known for many years. He seemed happy—but just as perplexed as I was.

Immediately, he reached into his top-left desk drawer and pulled out a sample of prenatal vitamins, instructing me to start taking them immediately. Walking across the room to get a cup of water for me, he pensively said, "You remember a couple of months ago when you had the cyst?"

"Yes," I said.

"The only thing I can think of is that something happened when the cyst ruptured. I don't know exactly how or why, but I do know an egg was released or you would not be pregnant."

He gave me a big bear hug when I got up to leave and told me to see the receptionist to schedule regular visits. When I walked into the waiting area, I could see my mother grinning from ear to ear. How did she know? She, too, gave me a giant hug and said, "Let's call Michael. He's been waiting to hear the news."

"What?" I queried.

"He's the reason I'm here," my mother said. "He called me earlier in the week and asked that I be with you, just in case."

About thirty minutes after leaving Texas Medical Center, we arrived at my apartment and called Michael. (We didn't have cell phones then). I dialed the number in Lubbock, and he picked up on the first ring.

"So what did the doctor say?" he asked, quickly followed by, "Was your mother there with you?"

"Yes, my mother was and is with me. And the doctor told me I'm going to have a baby."

"That's wonderful! I knew it in my heart," he exclaimed. We agreed to talk again later that evening.

Mom and I ran errands—getting my prescriptions filled, buying healthy foods from the grocery store, and finally relaxing at the apartment with a cup of my favorite jasmine green tea. Delicately, we sipped our tea out of fine Schumann Bavaria German china, looking at one another and giggling like schoolgirls as we talked about me being pregnant.

"When's your due date?" she asked. "Dr. Brown guesstimated May 3; wouldn't it be weird if my baby were born on the same day Granny died [May 17]?"

Granny was my maternal grandmother, Minnie, to whom I had been much closer than my mother. She had died in 1977, taking a piece of my heart with her. She had two daughters who had two daughters, and she had always wanted a boy. Maybe, just maybe, I would have that boy!

★ ★ ★

That night I headed to my bedroom, hoping to lay my head on the pillow and go to sleep. I was unable to articulate the feelings swirling around in my mind. What was happening? How? And *why?*

I was abruptly pulled back to reality by the ring of the phone. I knew it was Michael. I didn't know if I was really ready to talk, but my hand reached for the phone automatically, and I sounded a weak "Hello."

Part of me was happy to be talking to him, while another part was still somewhere else. He wanted a play-by-play of the visit to the doctor's office. He was concerned about how I was feeling physically and told me, somewhat dictatorially, that he would be arriving Friday on Southwest Flight 826. Professing his love for me, he said, "Good night, I'll see you this weekend."

I really loved Michael, and I felt excited that he would be back in Houston soon.

2

Lubbock

I had never quit anything in my life, so making the pressured decision to withdraw from my classes, leave work, and abort my life plan to move to Lubbock, Texas, was the most difficult thing I had ever done. I was prepared to stay the course, have the child on my own, and deal with life as it presented itself. But Michael insisted on us being together, and I caved in.

After saying our good-byes to family and friends, we packed and loaded the U-Haul hitched to my 1974 red, black-topped, two-door Monte Carlo. Thirteen hours later, we reached 19th Street and apartment F32—a small, dreary, one-bedroom apartment with the tiniest kitchen I had ever seen—which we would now call home. Of course, young love doesn't care about the size or functionality of living space. As long as we were together, we'd be happy, right?

On the bright side, Dr. Brown had referred me to his very good friend and colleague in Lubbock, Dr. Filipe—who welcomed me warmly and appeared delighted to have me as a patient. He wasn't Dr. Brown, but somehow, I felt comforted by the connection between the two doctors.

Michael had been living in Lubbock for about five months and was fairly well established in the community by then. Two of Michael's friends' wives were also pregnant—Jennifer was due three months ahead of me, in February, and Debbie was due three months behind me, in August. The three of us compared pregnancy notes all the time. We shopped, went to lunch, watched the guys' softball games, and gathered together with our spouses almost every weekend. All in all, I was enjoying being there, especially after we moved to a much larger two-bedroom, two-bath apartment. Now we could have our friends visit us. Life began to feel more settled.

My disappointment about having withdrawn from classes to make the move faded when I learned that the medical school at Texas Tech had recently opened and was accepting students who had not yet graduated. With good grades and a strong recommendation, a three-year undergraduate could get in—and I felt I could do it with the help of my University of Houston professors, of Dr. Filipe (who was affiliated with Texas Tech), and of several University of Texas Medical School contacts. If that didn't work out, I would just take courses to complete my bachelor's degree.

I planned to be there by spring. Since I wasn't working or going to school yet, I had plenty of time on my hands. Often I would walk around the Texas Tech campus familiarizing myself with the buildings, or I would get in the car and drive around to learn about the city and the surrounding area.

One day I decided to stop at the country club to get a sandwich—and I was shocked to see Michael sitting at the end of the bar in the middle of the day, drinking a beer. I stopped and observed him quietly for a few minutes. With several days' worth of stubble on his face and his head hanging down unnaturally, he looked downhearted and despondent.

I sensed it was best not to approach him, so I quietly backed up, retracing my footsteps one at a time. I silently exited the door I had entered just moments before.

3

Past Meets Present

In January, I enrolled as planned at Texas Tech, taking several of the classes that I had dropped at UH the prior fall semester. The baby was due in May, giving me plenty of time to complete the semester.

On one of my regular visits to Dr. Filipe, he was shocked and surprised to see that I had lost a significant amount of weight for five months' gestation. His concern was so great that he decided to hospitalize me to determine the cause. I was stupefied. I had never been pregnant before, and admittedly, I felt somewhat ignorant despite all the information I had gleaned from the various books I'd read. I'd thought I was fine, and I'd just stayed busy with school.

I had never been in a hospital other than to visit friends or relatives, and the reality of it didn't hit me until I was the one lying in the hospital bed. All I could hear, over and over again, was the message I had been given when I was sixteen: "The likelihood of you having a child is slim to none . . . the likelihood of you having a child is slim to none . . . the likelihood of you having a child is slim to none."

My feelings were all over the board as I lay there, my mind wandering. I sensed something was not "right" with Michael, but I couldn't put a finger on what it was. Part of me felt he was with me out of a sense of responsibility, despite his words of deep love for me. I reflected on how often he would lock himself in the bedroom and talk on the phone. He had a child, Christopher, by a previous marriage, so I assumed his conversations were with his son or the child's mother, Jane, and that he simply wanted privacy. Maybe he didn't want to upset me. Also, Michael and Jane's divorce was not final—a minor tidbit that he had failed to mention when we started dating and that he had not shared with me until I moved to Lubbock!

So not only did I feel vulnerable, but I also felt a strong survival instinct kicking in along with a sense of responsibility for my own situation and that of my unborn child. Could this be why I was losing weight? No, not possible, I deduced in the recesses of my nomadic thoughts. Was I fighting too hard to move forward educationally so I could take care of myself, just in case—no matter what? I deflected each of these thoughts as they surfaced, pushing them away somewhere—anywhere.

In the midst of the subtle relationship dynamics playing out between Michael and me, I felt blessed to have a little human being growing inside me. I sensed an unusual closeness to this little one, something unique and special—so much so that I tossed out all the "Name Your Baby" books and focused on names in the Bible. During my sleepless nights in the hospital, and then later at home, I pored through the Bible, page by page, writing names that I liked on a sheet of paper. I felt guided in some way, and I also felt peaceful inside. I wanted a boy—and I only selected male names from the Bible.

I was in the hospital for a week. Numerous tests were run, and each one came back normal. The baby was the exact size it should be for the gestation period. The fetus was getting all the nourishment it needed—but for some unknown reason, I was not getting what I needed to grow and thrive.

Not knowing exactly why I was losing weight, Dr. Filipe told me I'd be putting myself and the baby at risk if I chose to continue going to school. He believed the stress was more than my body could handle. He took the time to explain that while I could always go back to school, due to my health history, I might not always have the opportunity to have a child.

He told me I wasn't out of the woods because he didn't yet know the physiological cause of my weight loss. Despite "beefing me up" in the hospital, he was concerned that I wouldn't gain or even hold weight once I was released. He instructed me to eat foods with lots of calories—banana splits, hot rolls, butter, and literally anything else I wanted as long as it was loaded with calories. We were in a precarious situation if I could not gain weight.

My decision to quit school again was a no-brainer.

The next few months were difficult and uncomfortable for me, physically and emotionally. Michael asked me to marry him several times, and each time I told him, "Not now." Something just didn't feel right. Jokingly, I told him I couldn't stand in front of a minister and say "I do"—I'd have to say "I did"!

He continued his behind-closed-doors phone conversations—and it really started to wear on me. One day while he was at school, I decided to dig through the boxes he had stored in the closet. Why? I had no clue. But I found a picture of a blond-haired woman sitting on a playground swing with a blond-haired boy in her lap.

I was staring deeply at the photo, taking in every pixel, when suddenly the door behind me flung open with quite a force. The next thing I knew, Michael whisked the picture out of my hands, instructing me not to get into his things again. I hesitantly asked who the people in the picture were, to which he blandly responded, "Jane and Christopher."

He then looked me in the eyes and, gently rubbing my growing belly, said firmly, "Don't ever doubt me! I love you and our unborn child!" The picture did not look like Jane or Christopher to me (I had seen other photos of them), but for now, I decided to remain silent. I thanked him for loving me and said, "C'mon, let's go eat some calories. I want a banana split."

4

The Hero Arrives

The ride to Methodist Hospital was a quick fifteen minutes. Once I checked in, I was bummed that Dr. Filipe was not on call. But his partner, Dr. Rheinhold—the more humorous one of the two—was.

For twelve hours, I walked the hallways doing all I could to keep from having to lie down. Finally, the pain got severe enough for me to surrender and find my labor room.

Michael was pretty useless by this time. He was unable to help me breathe to stay on top of the pain, as we had been coached to do in our Lamaze classes. Thankfully, a nurse named Linda stepped in to assist me.

I had planned to have a natural childbirth, meaning I had opted not to have anesthesia of any kind. But after another three hours of close, hard contractions, I was completely wiped out. I had no stamina left, and no amount of breathing or mind focus on a spot on the wall helped. I no sooner breathed through one contraction than another was upon me—worse than the previous one. I pleaded for relief. Fifteen hours had passed with no end in sight, and I needed help.

Linda called an off-duty anesthesiologist, who agreed to come to the hospital to give me an epidural. By now it was about 3:00 a.m., and I was as limp as a dishrag.

The medication took effect and I rested peacefully for slightly over an hour until Dr. Rheinhold came in with a happy-sounding voice, saying, "Are you ready? Let's go deliver a baby."

Following Dr. Rheinhold's lead, I did well, and my baby was guided effortlessly into this world. It was the same day, the same hour, and almost the same minute when my maternal grandmother, Minnie, had died two years before!

Moving my thoughts from the clock to the sound of Dr. Rheinhold's voice, I heard him say, "Well, I won't have to circumcise this one."

"Is it a girl?" I asked.

"No, no it is not," he responded. Now I was really confused. Dr. Rheinhold was a jokester with a great sense of humor, but I didn't get it. (We would later learn that our son had *hypospadias*, a condition that requires that the foreskin be retained for reconstructive surgery later.)

I looked over at Michael and quickly asked, "What are we going to do? We don't have a girl's name picked out."

Dr. Rheinhold knew I really wanted a boy, and as he placed the child upon my breast, he said, "Here's your boy." Still somewhat confused, I began to cry as I held my baby boy close.

The baby I held in my arms was the child medical professionals told me I would never have! Born May 17, 1979, at 5:10 a.m. (CST) in Lubbock, Texas, weighing 7 pounds 9½ ounces and measuring 20 inches in length, Micah Aaron Matthew Felcman arrived to parents Mindy and Michael.

Tears flowed as I held this tiny new human close to my chest, heartbeat to heartbeat. He was tightly wrapped in a blanket like a papoose, and his body was warm. His breaths were quick and shallow, and suckling sounds were followed by an occasional grimace. He smelled like a newborn, and I sensed the comfort and feeling of safety he felt in his new world while in his mother's arms.

I sang to him and held him close, with tears of awe still flowing, knowing I would always be there for him. I would never leave or abandon this precious soul, this precious gift from God. I had been graced with motherhood, a job and role that I could not fail in. This tiny being needed me.

And so began the dance—two souls' journey of hardship and tragedy, challenge and growth, love and wisdom.

5

What's in a Name?

Two weeks after his birth, little Matthew made his first airplane ride from Lubbock to Houston for his introduction to other family members and friends. He was a natural traveler—no crying or fidgeting, just enjoying the first ride of his early life.

While on board, Michael and I continued our discussion about which of our child's names to call him. I pleaded for Micah, as the name was uncommon and I loved its meaning: "who is like Yahweh (God)." I explained, "Micah was an Old Testament prophet and writer whose work was directed more to the common people than to royalty and whose message was to live in a godly way and to have hope, no matter what happens."

I shared my knowledge of the other names as well. "Aaron was Moses' brother—three years older and a high priest. When the people were in real distress, Aaron had the job of atoning for their sins. He often spoke on behalf of Moses. Matthew is the most common name of the three. It is a shortening of the Biblical name Mattathias, which means 'the gift of God.'

"Matthew was a writer and a tax collector in the New Testament. Despite a sinful past, he was uniquely qualified to be a disciple of Jesus and displayed one of the most radically changed lives in the Bible in response to Jesus' invitation. Matthew did not hesitate, nor did he look back. He left behind a life of wealth and security for poverty and uncertainty. He abandoned the pleasures of the world for the promise of eternal life," I concluded.

Michael was astonished and impressed by the wealth of information I had retained regarding names. His primary concern about the name Micah was that people would confuse it with Michael. We practiced saying "Micah, Michael" over and over again, and ultimately, we agreed on Matthew for the time being. We believed that once our son was old enough to choose differently, he would select the name he wanted for himself anyway.

"Place your seats and tray tables in their upright, locked position and prepare for arrival in Houston," rang out over the PA system. I cradled little Matthew close to my body, gazing in awe at the holiness his power-packed tiny body held.

He was a gift from God, and he was a miracle!

6

Bound for Foreign Lands

For now I dropped the idea of going to medical school. Michael and I agreed to move back to Houston, where we would be closer to family and friends and I could complete my last year of undergraduate school. We were married on July 13, 1979.

Now that we had a family, Michael decided to drop out of school and return to working in sales and marketing of oil field equipment, which he had done before meeting me. He got a job at a company called Reed American. My mother agreed to keep Matthew while I went to school—an absolute godsend. Each day began at 4:00 a.m. with Matthew's first feeding, and it often ended as late as midnight, depending on my homework and test schedules. Every moment of every twenty-four hours was planned. But somehow I made the best grades I had ever made and graduated in May 1980—finally!

I still had medical school in my blood, so I got a job in the Cochlear Implant Laboratory at UT Medical School. But patient contact was minimal, and more laboratory work was not what I wanted, so I began poking around for other possibilities. Out of the blue, I was contacted by a retired Humble Oil-Exxon geologist, Robert Mason, who had formed an exploration and development company and needed help.

I told him that everything I had studied related to life science, not rocks—I was a biologist, not a geologist. He laughed at me, saying,

"Little lady, with the courses you've taken and the grades you've made, I can teach you what you need to know about oil and gas." Rather sheepishly, I responded, "OK," not knowing what impact that decision would have on the rest of my life.

Mr. Mason took me under his wing to teach me everything I could absorb. The first thing he insisted I do was attend drilling school—complete with hard hat, overalls, and steel-toed boots out in the field. I learned how to read well logs (to me it was just like an EKG read and calculated vertically rather than horizontally), spud, select bits, drill, set pipe, set casing, shoot, operate—literally everything from planning to production and beyond.

Once I was done with drilling school, I moved inside the office to learn the ins and outs of land work. I became the internal backstop for the outside land man, whose job was to make sure all legal documents were in order regarding land ownership and the oil, gas, and mineral interests for the properties we leased. As if that weren't enough, once I learned the basic mechanics of how to get oil and gas out of the ground, Mr. Mason decided it was time to teach me the business side. He taught me how to put oil-and-gas investment packages together and pitch them to potential investors, most of whom were sturdy, cowboy-hat-wearing, good ole boys who were the most intimidating people I had ever met.

Before sending me out alone to do these presentations, Mr. Mason took me along with him to observe. I will never forget my first solo pitch. Mr. Mason was absorbed with something more critical to him, so he sent me—at all of 23 years old and 104 pounds—to Longhorn Oil and Gas to convince a conference roomful of men that they needed to invest in our project. He told me not to come back without 100 percent participation!

The closer I got to their building, the harder my knobby knees rattled, and I thought I would collapse when I opened the door and felt the force of good-ole-boy group energy blaring right at me, just waiting for me to trip up on something so they could shred me to pieces and laughingly send me on my way.

Fortunately, I knew my stuff, handled myself well, and delightfully headed back to Mr. Mason with all participants on board, signed agreements in hand.

After two years of doing this work, I got bored, and I once again felt ready for medical school. Matthew was not nearly as needy as he had been as an infant, and I felt I could handle school much better now than I could when he was first born. I knew it would be a long road, but I had the loving support of family and close friends.

No sooner had I decided firmly that this would be my next step than Michael's company decided that they wanted to transfer him overseas. I raised holy hell and said, "Absolutely, no way! I have given up my dream long enough." I had already requested an application, and my references had all been contacted and stood ready to support my decision.

Michael took the news back to his boss, Alex, who instantly responded with, "Do you think she would be willing to go if we put her to work, too?" Michael came home from work that evening and told me of his surprise meeting with Alex. I responded with, "Are you kidding me? He's joking. If he were serious, he would talk to *me*, not you!"

The next morning, Alex called and invited Michael and me to dinner. Alex was a former GE executive who really knew the art of schmoozing. Definitely one of the good ole boys, he was nevertheless different from the others I'd encountered. I agreed to dinner. *What could it hurt?* I thought.

Alex painted the move as an opportunity. He had already planned what my role would be and how long I would need to train domestically before we moved to Singapore under a three-year contract. He added that I would still be young when we came back and that I could apply for medical school at that time.

I had tremendous skills in oil and gas that would be a huge asset for the company. Reed American, a division of Baker International, was losing market share in the Pacific Rim. To overtake the competition, the decision had been made to have a presence on the ground in the Far East. It was up to Alex to decide who that presence would be.

He sweetened the pot by saying our son would be young, would have wonderful experiences, and would be back by the time he started school. My head was spinning by the time dinner was over.

After a couple of weeks of deep consideration, Michael and I decided we were the ones to be the pioneers for Reed American on the ground in the Pacific Rim. My training began immediately, and as soon as it was completed, we were ready to go.

In early March 1982, Michael and I locked hands with Matthew—the three of us staring into each other's eyes and rapidly moving into the unknown as the Singapore Airlines 747 took off.

7

Surprises in Singapore

Approximately twenty-four hours after departure, we landed at Changi Airport in Singapore. Tired and smelling like the inside of an airplane, we hailed a taxi and directed the driver to the Hilton Hotel on Orchard Road—where we would stay for the next six to eight weeks. After showering, we struck out to explore the land that would be our home for the next three years.

An island nation, Singapore is approximately thirty miles long and sixteen miles wide at its widest point. With its lush tropical landscape and cosmopolitan Asian culture, it immediately became a place of great adventure for us.

Matt soaked up all of the attention he got from the Singaporeans. He was friendly and outgoing, and he adapted easily. The hotel personnel spoiled him completely! It seemed as if they were waiting for him to get off the "lift" each morning as we headed to breakfast, and they were always there to greet him each time we returned to the hotel from our outings.

I loved our new adventure. Often after house hunting, we explored the local markets, savoring the smells of spices in the air. We gawked at the open-air market, where you simply pointed to the chicken you wanted to buy and watched as it was promptly sacrificed with a quick snap of the neck, then placed in a centrifuge to spin off all the feathers. It was then cut into pieces, feet still on the drumsticks.

Venom was a common item of interest to the locals. Snakes—mostly cobras—were kept in grass sacks, and the vendor would toss them out into the aisle so a purchaser could point to the one he or she wanted to use! Imagine these deadly snakes slithering all over the place and local people simply stepping over them, should their paths cross.

The first time we saw this, all of us were flabbergasted. (Ain't seen nothin' like this in Texas—certainly not with rattlesnakes!) Little Matt was all eyes and ears. I watched intently as the vendor picked up the snake the purchaser had selected, held it behind the head, and milked its venom into a small piece of plastic that he then bound with a rubber band. He collected the money from the purchaser and then nonchalantly gathered the rest of the snakes and returned them to the grass sack. I later learned that many of the snakes in Singapore were deadly. Their venom was purchased for making antivenom, which many people kept on hand at home—just in case.

Farther down the aisle, Matt became fascinated with some caged live animals for sale. Locals told us they were "fruit bats" or "flying foxes." They were unique and interesting, their faces identical to that of a fox: ears; long nose; whiskers; and round, somewhat protruding brown eyes. Their bodies were bigger than that of the common black bat, but with foxlike, brownish-red hair. They hung upside down, and their wings were black, with a span of eighteen inches to two feet. They were remarkably friendly-looking creatures that our whole family felt blessed to experience.

One Saturday, after finding our new home, the three of us headed to the roof of the hotel to hang out by the pool. As the elevator doors opened, we were all surprised to see three Western-looking people on the elevator headed to the top, just as we were. We had become so accustomed to interacting with Singaporeans and people of other Asian nationalities that we were taken aback when we saw three people who looked like us!

We quickly discovered that the three of them were from Texas, too, and that they were another family, just like us, who had been transferred to Singapore. This family—Randy, Marty, and their son, Jason—would turn out to be wonderful friends and pivotal players in our lives for years to come.

★ ★ ★

The house we selected was in a local neighborhood. Our yard was large, peppered on one side with rambutan and chico trees. Bananas and bougainvillea grew wild along the fence line, and the driveway was long, paved, and gated—with tons of room for kids to play safely. The interior of the home was large enough to use one of the rooms for the initial Reed American office.

I began interviewing candidates for our *amah*—a live-in who cares for the children and helps with all the chores of running a household. This concept was brand-new to me and initially felt odd. However, it was how things were done there, and after several interviews, I selected a beautiful, wonderful Filipina named Anilee to become the newest member of our family.

Michael and I quickly settled into our respective work duties and responsibilities. We truly had fun together trying to figure out what we were doing. I attended telex school—there were no cell phones or personal computers in the early eighties—to learn how to communicate with our agents and customers in different time zones.

I had not turned twenty-five yet, and looking back, I was too young to realize the magnitude of what we had been tasked with. New adventures and challenges were fun for me, and this one gave me the opportunity to manage and run a business soup to nuts. Both of us were outgoing, athletic people, and we quickly developed a rather large circle of friends outside of business, too, whom we met primarily through softball and tennis. Life was exciting and loads of fun!

Matt turned three in May of that year. One night the three of us went to a local restaurant for dinner. The very kind waiter strategically placed Matt in a high chair between Michael and me and proceeded about his business. When the food arrived, Michael and I were astounded to hear Matt speak to the waiter in Mandarin—and to hear the waiter respond! We must have looked shocked because the waiter gently explained, "Sir, Madam, he asked for a fork." Michael and I looked at one another, shaking our heads and laughing.

Christopher, Michael's older son, came for a summer visit and ended up living with us. We were delighted to have him with us! I did everything I knew how to take care of, hold together, and please everyone in the family—something I guess all moms do.

Chris started first grade at Singapore American School; he rode a bus to and from school each day. Matt simply couldn't stand being left behind, so we decided to enroll him at Ulu Pandan, a local preschool nearby. He, too, rode a bus each day—and it nearly killed me to see him so little and yet trying to be so big, going to school. He could barely get up the steps on the bus, and often, Anilee would go with him because she couldn't stand to see him go off by himself, either!

At age three, Matt insisted the training wheels come off his little yellow bicycle because Christopher was getting his training wheels off. Matt had little concern for being three years younger, as he had already mastered balance and coordination a mere six weeks after getting his bicycle.

Michael and I decided early on that we would never be out of the country at the same time, so he did most of the traveling while I handled everything else from Singapore. The division of duties seemed to work well for us; at least one of us was always home with the boys. Our lives were great! We had tons of friends, traveled globally, shared experiences with the boys, and were very successful in the business.

Yet something inside me felt awkward. I couldn't get a grip on what it was, but it felt as if I had to do everything I could to keep Michael from leaving us. I had no clue why.

I noticed a California phone number showed up on our phone bill every time Michael traveled, no matter where he was or for how long. The number was not one I recognized, like the many others related to Baker International (Reed American's parent company).

But one day, while doing routine financial work and bookkeeping, a little voice inside me demanded that I pay attention to it.

On this particular day, the office was quiet; no one was around but me. I picked up the phone and dialed the number, the beat of my heart rapidly increasing with each ring. The voice that answered on the other end of the phone was that of a woman who simply said, "Hello."

In milliseconds my brain registered: *THIS IS NOT A BUSINESS! Whoa!* The adrenaline rush was in full swing. In a businesslike tone, I asked this woman if she or anyone at this number knew a man named Michael Felcman. She promptly responded, "Who wants to know?"

"Mindy Felcman," I stated in a bold tone, as if to stake my territory.

The next three hours of conversation shredded my perception of the previous five years of my life. Michael had been living a double life. Every time he'd had the opportunity, he'd called or visited this woman. She was Canadian, Roman Catholic, married—and had a child! And she'd had Michael's child, another son, one month after I found out I was pregnant.

Michael walked in on us near the end of the three hours and wanted to know whom I was talking to. With his mistress still on the line, I looked directly into his eyes and said, "Kathy Smith."

Michael's response—both physically and emotionally—was marginal at best. He stood in the doorway, dropping his head at the news and shaking it negatively. He had been caught red-handed in a very long, deep deception. I am not a screamer, a yeller, or a violent person, so I went inward, not outward. I needed to understand *why*.

Kathy agreed that if he ever tried to contact her again, she would inform me. She, too, had been deeply deceived.

For weeks after my discovery, I tried to process what had happened—until one day, I fainted. I woke up to bright lights, ammonia smells, and several strangers hovering over me. I was hospitalized for a week, unable to recall very little other than the fact that every time I woke up, I was given something to make me sleep again. My friend Marty kept vigil by my bedside, keeping visitors away and making up a story about why I was there. To this day, no one else in our very large social and business circle knows what happened.

Once I returned home, I had to figure out what I wanted to do and how I was going to do it. Unfortunately, I could not simply leave the country and go to America with my child. My heart bled for Christopher, and I felt I could not go off and leave him, either. Needless to say, I was in a pickle, and I had to figure out how to live in the situation I was in until I could get back to the United States.

The effects of the trauma continued. One day while grocery shopping, I lost part of my vision. I could see parts of the landscape before me, but other parts had large, gaping black holes in the field. I was frightened, thinking I had had a reaction to the medicines I'd been given in the hospital. I froze in my footsteps for over ten minutes before my vision began to return. When it did come back, I had an excruciating, pounding headache.

Michael and I kept my hospitalization and our relationship troubles to ourselves and continued life one day at a time. Mentally, I set small one- to three-month timelines to get me through the nine months left on our contract. Work, tennis, and the children's activities kept me occupied, although it was difficult at times when Michael was traveling, knowing what he might be up to. I tried to understand why this had happened, what had caused it, and whether understanding it might give us a chance.

But I now had zero trust in him. All the fun I had experienced in Singapore was now tainted by a heaviness that made it very difficult for me to live as openly and happily as I had before. I was severely traumatized emotionally, with no support or help to recover, so I learned to live by my survival instincts.

I really loved Michael, but I began to doubt everything I knew about myself. Would he have done this if I had been good enough? Pretty enough? Smart enough? Self-doubt nagged at me as I desperately tried to understand why this had happened.

8

Back in Houston: A Boy's Cry for his Father

The Singapore mission was a complete success. We turned a large cost center into a $3 million profit center and passed it over to the locals to run—all within a three-year period. It felt good to have this achievement under our belts.

But once back in Houston, it became clear that the oil and gas industry was in serious decline. Inflation was high, and interest rates were in the double digits. Michael still had a job with Reed American, and with the laurels of our Singapore assignment, I landed a job in economic development with the Scottish Development Agency, a branch of the government of the United Kingdom.

The boys went to school three blocks from the house, and everything seemed to be OK. They resumed their sports activities, and I continued my mom duties, going to as many of the kids' games as possible. When Michael was in town, he participated in their games, too. Sometimes, one of us would attend Matt's game while the other attended Christopher's. Then, midway through, we would switch, and we'd all meet somewhere after the games.

Given the "elephant in the room" between Michael and me, I decided to go back to the University of Houston to pursue a master's degree in business—another paper chase to qualify me to do what I had been doing for the past three years. After all, a degree in biology had not imparted much about how to do international business—and my dream of medical school drifted further and further away.

Michael continued to travel for long periods of time, often returning only to disturb the routines the boys and I had settled into. Helping with homework, talking to the kids about the birds and the bees, attending Cub Scouts, getting them to their sports activities, and refereeing neighborhood or playground altercations—that all landed on my shoulders. My perception that Matthew and Christopher needed me kept me in the relationship with Michael.

My heart hurt most for Christopher, whose mother had given up custody of him when she decided to remarry and whose father was often unavailable emotionally—and living a double life. At least Matthew had me (the part of me that wasn't consumed with Michael and my efforts to become independent of him), but I'm not even sure I was what Matt really needed.

Though barely able to write, Matt one day pulled a sheet of paper out of his backpack, telling me he had written something for his father and wanted to show it to him when he returned home. Tears rolled down my cheeks, dropping softly onto the paper as I read the heartfelt expression of a child not yet six years old.

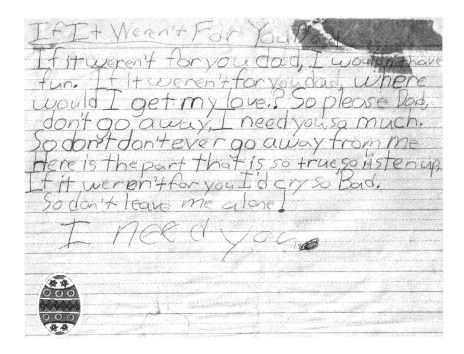

If It Weren't For You
If it weren't for you dad, I wouldn't have
fun. If it weren't for you dad, where
would I get my love? So please Dad,
don't go away, I need you so much.
So don't don't ever go away from me
Here is the part that is so true, so listen up,
If it weren't for you I'd cry so Bad,
So don't leave me alone!
I need you

* * *

Somewhere along the way, Michael began referring to Christopher as his "number-one son." He only meant that Christopher had been born first, but little Matthew interpreted the words to mean that he wasn't as good as Christopher—and might not ever be. He desperately wanted and needed his father's undivided attention.

It is difficult to describe how I felt about Michael. I still didn't trust him, but I did manage to feel a small degree of compassion for him. Unclear about how I would proceed in the relationship, I decided to give him a chance, continue with my short one- to three-month goals, continually reassess our relationship, and be willing to move on if the environment became unbearable.

Unfortunately, neither of us was aware of family counseling services, so we continued living as if we were asleep. Our social life was extremely active, and as usual, no one—including immediate family members—knew of the difficulties our family was experiencing.

My headaches and vision problems continued, becoming more frequent and much more severe. Often, the pain was so intense that I would vomit.

I was accepted into the MBA program at the University of Houston, and I felt excited to begin night classes starting in the upcoming spring semester. However, the frequency of the headaches increased, and I became concerned I might not be able to go to school. I went to see Dr. Brown, knowing full well his specialty was the "other end" but also knowing that he cared about me and could help me. He referred me to a South African neurologist nearby, one who was well aware of the seriousness of migraines—his face was permanently distorted as a result of having severe migraines himself.

One day, while visiting the neurologist, my hand began to tingle, and I showed him how it became splotchy in shades of red and white. Immediately, he identified the source of my migraine headaches as a vascular problem connected more to my heart than my head. He gave me a prescription for Procardia and I have not had a migraine headache since. My heart had been broken, and my physical body had revealed it!

★ ★ ★

One night, not long after the boys went to bed, I was awakened by blood-curdling screams coming from Matt's room. I blasted up the stairs and found him red-faced, crying, and scared to pieces. "What happened?" I questioned, as I picked him up and held him close to my body, feeling his heart race and his body tighten. "Did you have a bad dream? Did your brother hit you? Did you fall out of bed?" Still sobbing, he shook his head no. I was grasping. I had no idea what had happened, but I stayed with him until he fell asleep.

This pattern continued with some frequency. He could not tell me what happened to cause this frightening experience—but the doctor did. Matt was diagnosed with allergy-related asthma, and I was taught what to do in case of emergency: inject him with epinephrine to get him to breathe and give me enough time to get him to a hospital. This was a very serious condition—it was life threatening. I had to remain calm, cool, collected, and responsive—not reactive—anytime his breathing was compromised. The episodes usually occurred in the night, so this mother's ear became highly attuned to the sound of Matt's breathing and any irregular rhythm during the night. Whether he was down the hall from me or upstairs, no sound escaped me.

In early 1986, Michael came home from work one day and told me he'd been contacted by a headhunter for a job in Boulder, Colorado. He'd been recruited to do the same type of work he had done in the oil and gas industry—but for a product that had multiple industry applications. His argument in favor of taking the position was that it was not tied to the rig count and was therefore a much more versatile, far-reaching opportunity. They wanted Michael for his expertise in building and developing international sales.

I felt angry! I wanted to be sought after for my expertise, too, but I was too busy trying to hold the family together. I sensed Michael would get this job, and now what was I supposed to do?

I was right. I had started night classes at the University of Houston and was continuing to work when sure enough, Michael was offered the job in Boulder.

Immediately, I began applying to universities in the Boulder and Denver areas in hopes of continuing my education and holding the family together in Colorado. I entertained staying in Houston with the children if I didn't get accepted in Colorado.

Fortunately, later in the spring, I received acceptance letters from every university I had applied to. I had the feeling we wouldn't be there long enough for me to complete the three-year MBA/JD program in international business that I was particularly interested in, so I opted for the two-year executive MBA program.

As soon as school was out for the summer, we made the long drive to Boulder in search of a new home and another new start in life.

9

Boulder: Landlocked

For all of the beauty and grandeur of the Rocky Mountains and the outdoorsy, active lifestyle, I knew my time in Colorado would be short-lived. I felt landlocked—literally and figuratively trapped. I made the most of my situation and tried to enjoy the ride for all it offered. But the altitude and the beautiful surroundings could not replace the peace I always felt when on or near the sea.

Nevertheless, Boulder and the surrounding areas were gorgeous. Once again, the boys started a new school—only this time, they were at different locations. Again, they had to make new friends and adjust to differences in school curriculums, but getting involved in sports helped them make the shift.

I started school in August 1986, working full-time during the day and going to school four nights a week year-round, from 6:00 p.m. to 10:00 p.m. On weekends I had school projects or homework to do with my study group. I worked for Citigroup and occasionally traveled to Chicago or New York for training. Every moment of my life was scheduled.

Michael continued traveling and could be away six to eight weeks or more at a time, usually in some remote part of the globe—no place he could return from quickly if needed. The boys and I were used to this schedule, but what was different this time was my absence four nights a week and often on weekend days as well. The boys would be sound asleep when I got home, and in the mornings, our time was short.

We learned to make the best of it. I drove to and from Denver each day, returning to Boulder close to 11:00 p.m. four nights a week. During winter months, I could arrive home much later if I got caught in a whiteout. Fortunately, I had a wonderful nanny and friends who were at the house after school to be with the children until I got home each evening.

And the guys Michael played rugby with were always there to help out if we needed them. When Michael was in town, it felt like Grand Central Station. He ran 5k fun runs with Matt, took the boys to his rugby practices and games, and planned and hosted frequent weekend parties. Our social network grew quickly once again.

Relationship issues were put on the back burner, especially with the length and frequency of Michael's travels and the intensity of my school schedule. The distance between us—and the difference in our focuses—seemed good for us. But the impact on the boys may have been a different story.

The New Year began with a fierce start. Once again, every minute of my schedule was planned, and I pleaded with Michael to cut his travels short for the sake of our family. Given my schedule, there had to be a way to shorten his extended periods of time away so he could be home with the boys more. I was working very hard to become a significant financial contributor to the family, and I wanted to be financially independent in case Michael and I ended up splitting up. At one point, Michael made the comment, "If something happened to us, you would be just fine."

"Yes, I would," I stated simply—and I meant it.

★ ★ ★

Matt loved to play with insects. He'd catch bumblebees by their wings, studying them intently to learn how they were made, and then he'd release them. (Had I done that as a child, I would have been stung and swollen beyond recognition.) He also liked to dig for worms and catch grasshoppers, crickets, and other crawling critters to go fishing with. He had a little red bucket, commonly referred to as his "fishing bucket," which he wandered off with whenever he was hell-bent on fishing.

By now, he did not have to ask every time he wanted to walk over to the lake to fish. His routine was simple: hunt for bait, walk over to the lake, catch the fish, then visit Irene. Irene was one of our neighbors, a widowed Irishwoman who took the time that I did not have to talk to Matt about his fishing expeditions and bait hunts. The two of them developed quite a rapport, so no matter the size of the fish he caught, she always cooked it (or them), and then the two of them would sit together and eat.

Yes, all it took was one tiny fish, and their ritual ensued. She threw in pieces of fruit or cheese, but she never failed to attend to his needs. If he disappeared for too long, I'd step out on the deck and peer two houses over—and see the two of them on her porch, talking and dining. I felt blessed to have such a loving, caring neighbor. I was so stressed with school and work that I could hardly function, much less take the tender time Irene did to meet Matt in his world.

One afternoon, while I was studying for exams, Matt came rushing into the kitchen, placed his red bucket dead center on the round table I was working on, and made a beeline to the bathroom. I heard a noise coming from the bucket but thought nothing of it, assuming he had caught a couple of bream. Head down, I continued my studies.

Then, unexpectedly, I heard a loud thud on the table— and right before me, a snake was crawling across my open book, headed directly toward me. I pushed my chair back with such force that I started falling over, screaming, "MMMMAAAAATTTTTTHHHHHEEEEWWWW!" on the way down.

He casually walked back into the kitchen with his pants around his ankles, and I yelled, "Get that snake out of here!"

"Oh, Mom, it's just a garter snake; it won't hurt you," he said, as I picked myself up off the floor and he pulled his britches up.

"I don't care what kind of snake it is; just get it out of this house!"

That was Matt, my nature boy, fearless beyond reason when it came to critters.

★ ★ ★

I was doing extremely well in business school, and at Citicorp, I was the top candidate selected to lead Credit Analysis for the newly formed health-care specialty area. What a great avenue to integrate my interests in medicine with business—and I'd get to move back to Texas!

As soon as I shared my news with Michael, however, I learned that he'd been in talks with his company about moving to the Middle East as soon as I graduated. Their plan was to have him on the ground in the center of his territory rather than having him cover it from Boulder. I was livid. I had not worked myself into the ground to follow him and his career around the globe. Inside, I was a basket case. The Middle East, of all places—the least woman-friendly working environment on the planet!

Here I was *again*, faced either with following my heart's desire and path or breaking up our family. Those were the only two possibilities that my "monkey mind" could conceive. *Why, God? Why is this happening again?*

Why had I hung onto this relationship only for these great divides to keep showing up? Is this what marriage was? More to the point, was hanging on—no matter how painful or damaging—really love? Would this compromise turn out be a chrysalis that would eventually lead to something wonderful and beautiful?

I had no clue.

10

Dubai: A Perfect Life

I was in so much turmoil that my supervisor finally asked me if something was wrong. I had not wanted to do anything to jeopardize my future opportunity with Citi, but I felt I had to confide in him.

Surprisingly, he promised to do what he could to help me. And one day when I least expected it, his supervisor called me into his office to let me know that he had arranged through the New York office for me to have exploratory interviews with several executives in the Dubai office. He hoped this would help me make the decision about whether or not to go with Michael. I felt happy and valued.

Now that getting work there was a possibility, I decided to go with Michael to Dubai to have a look-see. I was delighted to learn that Citi in Dubai was interested in me for a position in risk management for the Middle East. This opportunity felt so much more intriguing to me than leading Credit Analysis at the new health-care division in Dallas.

I graduated in June, and by early August, our family was in Dubai. Two days after our arrival, I went to the bank to meet the folks I would be working with—only to learn that the whole division had been moved to Bahrain—an island country in the Arabian Gulf along the eastern coastline of Saudi Arabia! Why hadn't anyone told me? The job was still mine if I wanted it, and Bahrain was only a three-hundred-mile plane ride away. But becoming a commuter in the Middle East was not an option, especially for a foreign expatriate female. Even more important, I needed more than a day and a half per week with my family. Now what?

Dubai in 1988 was an unheard-of locale—not the glamour spot it is today. Something about it in its old days was attractive to me—it felt as if I'd been there before. The pace of life was slow. The terrain was desert as far as the eye could see. Driving down the road, one could see camels, hobbled so they couldn't wander too far from their master, eating out of old school barrel cans used to burn trash. Locals dressed in *dishdashas* and *abayas*. A smile and a wave of the hand were commonplace.

Our move to Dubai was nothing like the move to Singapore in that a home was awaiting us when we arrived. There were no extended hotel stays, and there was no time spent searching for a place to live. The whole family was in heaven because our home was right on the Arabian Gulf—the beach was right outside our front door!

At school, the boys were once again the new kids on the block. But this was common in an international school, so they didn't stand out as they would have stateside. All of the children were subject to relocation at any time, and they had a respect for one another that was not often experienced in their home countries.

Michael and the boys got settled at work and in school, respectively—while I sat and wondered what I would do with my life for the next three years. Women typically just didn't work in Dubai—especially expatriate women who were there with their husbands. Here I was with a brand-new MBA and Fortune 500 experience—and nothing to do with them!

Jim Helmsworth, our next door neighbor and Michael's co-worker, was the first to tell me that my chances of getting a job were slim. After two years, he knew the lay of the land—and he discouraged me from even looking. He suggested that I have Payton, his wife, introduce me to her friends and that I start my new life in Dubai as an expatriate wife: golf, the Petroleum Wives' Club, bridge clubs, etc. I agreed to meet as many people as I possibly could, but "expatriate wife" was merely one possibility as far as I was concerned (and not at the top of my list).

I thanked Jim for his genuine efforts to guide me, but I proceeded to seek out what I knew I needed to do. Immediately I began networking—first with banks, then with oil and gas companies.

My fourth networking meeting was with the regional manager of Reading and Bates, an American named Ken Franzier. The company's banking relationship in Dubai was with a British bank. Ken picked up the phone while I sat there, and he contacted his bank officer to schedule an appointment for me.

Later that day, I was on the twenty-eighth floor of the World Trade Centre Building in Dubai, meeting with a gentleman named Alan Johnston. I left the meeting feeling pretty good—I'd been confident and knowledgeable about the topics we had discussed.

I had not been home two hours when the phone rang. It was Alan, asking if I could come in the next morning to meet the general manager of the bank, Jonathan Nail, and the assistant general manager, Ralph Stockton. My heart raced. Yes, I could come in at ten o'clock Tuesday morning. When I hung up, the boys wanted to know why I was jumping up and down so much. I was so excited that I ran next door to tell Payton and Jim. Michael was supportive but unemotional.

There was no way to formally prepare for a meeting of this kind. They had my résumé and had been debriefed by Alan. My job was to be myself.

I arrived ten minutes ahead of schedule and sat patiently in the bank lobby. I was quickly called into the same conference room I had sat in the day before with Alan. I met individually with Mr. Nail and Mr. Stockton, then with both of them together. At the end of the meeting, they said they would contact me in a couple of days.

Sure enough, they did. They had a definite offer but asked me to come in again—they wanted me to be part of its creation prior to making it formal. Jim couldn't believe it! In a mere two weeks, I had become the head of corporate Credit and Marketing—an American female in an executive role at a British bank in the Middle East!

Professionally, it was a quantum leap. I was also happier with my work than I had ever been. I was a phenomenon—on the cutting edge of change. I had responsibility for the nine countries in the Middle East where the bank did business. And while I didn't personally travel to all those regions, I guided the efforts of the men who did.

After a few months, I decided to run for a seat on the Board of Directors of the American Business Council, which was part of the US Chamber of Commerce. Once again, Jim kindly counseled me that this group was all male and that I shouldn't be disappointed when I wasn't voted in. Gobsmacked (my favorite British expression for "astonished") again! I won the position by a landslide, and I was the only woman in the whole organization.

As part of this role, it was my job to lobby Congress once a year for US business interests in the Middle East. Numerous affluent locals supported my efforts, dubbing me an "ambassador of goodwill" for their country. Whenever I was on the Hill, it took little effort to meet with any senator or representative, including Geraldine Ferraro, the first female vice-presidential candidate in history to represent a major political party.

Very simply, the congressmen and congresswomen were captivated by me—although they were usually more curious to know how I had obtained my position than to know what I was lobbying for. The bank supported me in this role, ensuring that each time I traveled to the United States, I met with the people at the multinational companies I managed. Numerous magazine and newspaper articles were written about me during this time, and Michael soon came to be referred to as "Mr. Mindy Felcman."

The bank asked that I volunteer to teach business mathematics at the women's school in Dubai as a way to give back to the local community. I loved teaching, and this gave me an opportunity to better understand the role of women in that culture. Some spoke exceptional English, and some spoke none. Although I studied classical Arabic, I had nowhere near the fluency level needed to teach in Arabic, so I asked for—and was given—a translator so that all the women could understand and take from my lessons exactly what they needed.

I had never had as much fun in my life as I had during my days in Dubai. I had three separate wardrobes: one for work, one for all the formal events I was required to attend, and one for my days off. On several occasions, I was asked to model for local designers, squeezing in lunchtime shows or late-night events. I love getting dressed up, so when it worked with my schedule, I was happy to oblige.

The formal work week in the Middle East is from Saturday morning through 2:00 p.m. on Thursday, with Friday being the holy day, much like Sunday in other parts of the world. The workday was from 8:00 a.m. to 2:00 p.m., then from 4:00 p.m. to 7:00 p.m. That's why evening events and dinner would often begin as late at 10:00 p.m. Imagine being in the money business with only three-and-a-half days overlapping with the rest of the world's financial markets.

In my early negotiations, I had asked to work the hours the boys were in school so I could be home to help them with homework, participate in their after-school activities, and get dinner started so they could eat at the times they were used to. Dinnertime was when our family shared the day's activities or anything that was on our minds. The arrangement worked well because the boys could have baths and be in bed by the time I might have to leave for a late-night bank event. If no events were on the schedule, then we had long evenings together.

When we had dinner parties or other events at our home, the boys were always included. They learned to set a formal table, display superior manners for their ages, and appropriately converse and engage in dialogue with our international and American guests.

I was happy for the first time in years. I was in my element—work was fun and exciting, and the boys were happy and doing well in school and their sports activities. Michael was happy with his job—still traveling, but not as much as he had done from the states, affording our family more time together.

But all that would change.

11

First Losses

The summer before moving to Dubai, Christopher spent a month with his mother, Jane. Her maternal instincts were reactivated, and she decided she wanted to have Christopher back. She planted the seeds of that with him during his visit and watered them every time she talked to him on the phone in Dubai.

The child was absolutely torn to pieces, as was I when I learned how accommodating Michael was being with her. God bless Jim Helmsworth! He agreed with me that it was Michael's place to put his foot down and tell Jane that under no circumstances would our family be broken up at her whim.

But Michael didn't, and while I would never stop a child who truly wanted to be with his or her mother, I had grave reservations about Christopher returning to live with his mother. I felt he was being bounced around too much and needed the stability that living with us gave him. But despite intense conversations with Michael and long nights of crying, Christopher, at age 13, left our family to go live with the mother who had abandoned him earlier in his life.

While I can't speak for Michael, Matt and I felt a deep hole. Michael continually asked me to stay in my bedroom when the hurt was so bad and the tears were so great that I couldn't manage them. He didn't want Matt to see me like "that." If I felt this bad, how was this impacting Matt? If my expression was being shut off, then by default, Matt's was too. I know he felt very much alone. His big brother was gone—perhaps forever.

I could feel the questions practically oozing from the pores of Matt's skin—questions that his little ten-year-old mind didn't dare articulate: Did Chris leave because of me? Did I do something wrong to make him leave? Will I ever see him again? Nowhere did he feel whole. For the first time in his life, he had to go to school alone. Chris was gone from school, from home, and from sports. My heart ached for Matt.

As Matt and I dealt with the loss as best we knew how, we seemed to grow closer. Michael also started engaging more with Matt, taking him to Cyprus and Israel while I was in London for two weeks. Matt befriended a new kid from Texas, Justin, who had just moved to Dubai and started at the Jumeirah American School where Matt went. Matt could readily relate to being the new kid, and now he had his own first new relationship since Christopher's departure.

★ ★ ★

On Fridays it was customary for me to work out and then go to the pool or beach with Michael and Matt. One Friday, Michael and Matt were already at the pool, and I was around the corner in the gym. It was a quiet, normal Friday until Matt burst into the gym screaming, "Mom! Dad needs you! A kid is drowning! Hurry, Mom, hurry!"

I rounded the corner and saw Michael and one of our neighbors, Glenn, a scuba diver, frantically doing CPR on a small limp body. As soon as I arrived, Michael backed away, and I stepped in. Glenn and I worked in synchrony, just as we had been taught as rescue divers. I looked at this cold, purple, little body and began mouth-to-mouth resuscitation, breathing every bit of life I could into his tiny lungs. At one point, he coughed and spit water.

Someone in the crowd called for emergency help while Glenn and I remained fast at work. *"Never stop cardio pulmonary resuscitation efforts until professional help arrives"* kept playing in my mind. At one point, I came up for air and asked where the parents were. Something in me felt that Glenn and I were missing something important. Unfortunately, no one surfaced.

At least thirty minutes passed before we heard the roar of a helicopter approaching. Glenn and I continued CPR as we carried the little body out to a table on the beach—anything to get closer to the professional help on the way. But the child showed no further signs of recovery. The pilots fumbled around the tail of the helicopter to get a gurney, wasting precious moments. What were they doing? Why were they wasting time?

Once the medics finally got to the table where Glenn and I were still working on the limp little body, they pushed us out of the way. They covered the child's mouth and nose with a green, bulbous mask—inflating the child's abdomen each time they squeezed the bulb. No air was getting into the lungs! What the hell were they doing? Where was the automated external defibrillator? The epinephrine? How archaic was a damn mask for a drowning incident that had occurred at least thirty minutes prior? I screamed again, "Where are the parents of this child?" Still no answer.

The helicopter lifted off, and I collapsed to the ground. I already knew this little one was dead. What I didn't know was that Matt was the one who had found him inches underwater, eyes fixated upward, and then pulled him out onto the bank. Matt had run over to Michael, who was sitting with Glenn, and had cried out to them to help the little boy. He had then courageously made his way to the gym to call me to the scene.

Hours later we got a call from the hospital. The professionals had gotten no more than a teaspoon of water out of the child's lungs. The family lived in Chicago Beach Village, but we didn't know them. The mother had left her son and a visiting friend at the pool while she ran to the store two blocks away. The little boy with reddish-brown curly hair and blue eyes was three years old, from Ireland—and he had asthma.

I *knew* there was something else we could have done! Merely steps away, I had epinephrine in the refrigerator for my own child with asthma. Numerous times I had had to use it to get him breathing. Had the parents been there with this information, this child could have been saved.

I never met nor heard from the parents of this little boy, but Matt was befriended by his older brother, Aeden. I remember answering the knock at the door the day Aeden asked to see Matt. While they attended different schools, once they finished their homework each afternoon, the two of them hung out together until near dark. I know they connected in the place of the deep emotional trauma of losing a brother. Aeden represented the big brother Matt had lost, and Matt represented the little brother Aeden had lost.

Such deep hurt and pain for such young boys.

12

The Drawings

One day in January 1990, while picking up and cleaning Matt's room, I discovered a folded piece of drawing paper that screamed at me to open it. I felt a bit odd, but the little voice inside of me insisted I was not being nosy or betraying my son's privacy. Opening the last fold, I stood in shock as I stared at the drawings of my ten-year-old son.

The page had multiple drawings on it, all with the same theme—death and self-destruction: a stick figure jumping off the pier with a ball and chain on one leg; a figure holding a pistol to the mouth; an arm with a syringe sticking into it; a wrist slashed by a knife; a figure in a chair with the words "high voltage" and a strap on the figure's arms; a stick figure jumping off a tall building; a face with a stick of dynamite on its nose; and the image of a face with hands choking the neck, the word "red" written in a bubble pointing to the face.

I don't know how long I stood there in the center of his room, flaccid until my brain registered the seriousness of the images on the page I held in my hand. I had to do something about this immediately.

Matt was outside playing when Michael arrived home. I handed him the folded paper. Shaking his head sadly, he agreed we had to act rapidly.

I called my friend Lynn, who had lived in Dubai for over ten years, to find out what she knew about the availability of psychiatrists, psychologists, and counselors. Unfortunately, at that time, the culture of the Middle East did not support these professions for an expatriate community. In their culture, it was commonplace for family members with these kinds of problems to be kept at home, away from the public. However, Lynn knew of a woman who had been a counselor in Denmark, and she agreed to meet with Michael, Matt, and me.

I was so far out of my league with this that I had no clue what to do, how to act, or what to expect. Thus far, I had not let Matt know that I had found the drawings. I just told him we were going to talk to a lady from Denmark who might be able to help us with the sadness we had about Christopher leaving. I had no clue if that was really what was bothering him, but I had to grab onto something that could make sense for him—and me!

Surprisingly, this woman, Lilly, lived in our neighborhood three streets behind us. The four of us sat in her living room, a mirror image of ours but with different furniture. Unfortunately, Lilly was "leading" in her assessment of Matt's drawings, coming off as accusatory rather than allowing him to explain them, which caused him to shut down. Matt's response to our visit with Lilly was that he never wanted to go back there again!

The only thing I knew to do next was ask friends back in Boulder to help me find a child psychologist with whom I could make a phone appointment. I needed to get back to the United States to someone who spoke the same language and had the same cultural protocols as we did, as quickly as possible. Fortunately, within a week, I had a phone consultation, and the next day, Matt and I were on a plane to Dr. Schanning's office in Boulder, Colorado.

I had no idea what I was heading into, nor did I know how long we would need to be there. The bank was more than supportive, instructing me to take as long as I needed. For me as a mother, this was the toughest thing I had ever experienced. I felt lost and helpless.

★ ★ ★

We spent several weeks in Boulder, sometimes seeing Dr. Schanning twice a day. Some of the visits were one-on-one, while others were with the two of us together. Dr. Schanning shared with me that he found Matt to be extremely enraged and significantly depressed. He believed the condition to be chronic, and brief crisis intervention or short-term hospitalization would not help the root cause.

He suggested two to four months of residential care or medium-term day treatment, neither of which was an option in Dubai. I could stay in Boulder somewhere while Matt went to such a facility, but how would I keep my job in Dubai and live the happy life I had just discovered? I considered taking a leave of absence and finding something nearby for a few months.

Michael showed no interest in moving back, and frankly, he was of little help in the decision-making process. I asked the doctor what he felt the impact of Matt's and my living away from Michael and our home would be if we decided to stay in Boulder for two to four months. He responded neutrally, letting me know that there was nothing magical about two to four months—it could be longer. There was no way to know.

I have often reflected on this crossroads in my life, wondering how things might have turned out if I had chosen differently. I had resisted moving to Dubai in the first place, and now I was faced with a decision I do not believe I was psychologically capable of making. My life was happier in Dubai, but now my child was in serious distress—and none of the options felt right. Dr. Schanning witnessed my anguish but insisted he couldn't tell me what to do; he merely made a professional recommendation based on an evaluation independent of the extenuating circumstances.

Matt and I returned to Dubai.

★ ★ ★

Why was I so driven to keep the family together? Was it because of someone else's belief system that had been instilled in me earlier in life? Was it my longing for connection? Was I trying to prove that Michael really hadn't married me out of a sense of responsibility? Was it my way of doing what I thought was necessary to take care of my child? Or was I just in denial about what Matt really needed?

I maintained close contact with Matt's teachers, kept a watchful eye on him, and had Lilly to help me out on occasion. Everyday life seemed to move along OK, although I had believed it to be OK before all of this happened, too. I really did not know what I was dealing with, and for whatever reason, I remained somewhat asleep.

13

Mauritius: Stranded

Michael asked if Matt and I would like to go with him to Mauritius, an island nation in the Indian Ocean off the southeast coast of Africa, to hang out while he worked. Matt was out of school, and given the stress I had recently experienced, I was ready for a respite.

To reach Mauritius, we had to travel first to London, then down to the Seychelles, and finally to our destination of Port Louis. We were fascinated by the beauty of the island—and even more so by the people. Mauritius had an interesting history that we had apprised ourselves of before landing.

At one time, the island was called Isle of France, but now the populace was composed of many ethnicities—people of Indian, African, French, and Chinese descent. Most Mauritians, though not all of them, were multilingual—speaking English, French, Creole, and Chinese. Being able to communicate in English depended on where we were and what we were doing.

Michael spent most of the days at the sugar plantations, while Matt and I spent our time exploring. Matt and I were very close during these times, in a way that's difficult to describe in words; we were two kindred souls, one playing the role of mother and the other that of child.

One day while we were out exploring, I was reminded that Mauritius had been the only home in the world of the now extinct dodo bird. I had a story to share with Matt about my childhood dodo-bird experience in Liberty, Texas. When I was in the fourth grade, I did a report on this creature, and when I presented it orally to my class, I called it a "doo-doo" bird. The whole class broke into laughter—I didn't know whether to laugh or cry. I was so embarrassed!

But the teacher kindly said, "Mindy, I believe it is pronounced 'do-do,' with a long *o* sound." Rapidly trying to save face, I corrected the pronunciation. I shared with Matt that the whole reason I had done the report on this bird in the first place was that I thought it was a doo-doo bird. Matt got tickled and broke out laughing. Hearing him laugh, I got tickled, and together we let out giant belly laughs as we walked the streets of Port Louis. We couldn't look at each other without cracking up!

Early the next morning, Michael left for the sugar plantation as usual. His meetings were going very well, and it looked as if he had successfully discovered another market application for the process-control instrumentation his company manufactured. Matt and I said our good-byes to Michael for the day. I made a pot of coffee, and Matt went out the sliding back door. I told him to stay on the grounds nearby and not go to the beach without me.

Suddenly, I heard a blood-curdling scream coming from the outside yard: "Mmmmoooooommmmmm, come here! Hurry!" Matt had found an iguana resting on the wall behind the hedge, right outside our room. This was the first time either of us had seen an iguana in its native habitat. Matt was spellbound, closely watching its every move.

I poured a cup of coffee and sat down on the lawn nearby. I was fascinated watching Matt and the iguana. It was as though the two of them were communicating in some way. After a while, I began reading my book. A short time later, Matt walked up. Looking up at him, I saw his tanned skin peeking out of his mauve-colored T-shirt against the backdrop of the multiple blue shades of the sky and the ocean—and a vibrant green lizard hanging from his earlobe, dangling like an earring. It was an image I will never forget. That child never ceased to amaze me with his critter antics.

It was impossible for me not to laugh, and when I did, the cycle of our belly laughs began all over again, until we decided it was time to go put on our swimsuits and head for the beach. He gracefully dislodged the small green reptile and placed it gently on the bush near the iguana.

The beach was topless, which didn't faze Matt one bit. Nothing stopped him from investigating the sands and the beautiful ocean waters. He loved snorkeling and exploring the critters of the sea as much as he did those of terra firma.

The day before, I had resurrected my windsurfing skills and had spent the majority of the day flying through the waves with the wind blowing in my face. But today, I stayed on the beach to read my book, peering out every other word to check on him. Every once in a while, we'd wave to each other, signaling that everything was OK.

This continued for at least an hour, when suddenly I noticed that rather than waving, Matt seemed to be motioning frantically for me. From my vantage point, it didn't appear that he had moved, so why was he waving for me to come? I thought perhaps he had found another creature that mesmerized him as much as the iguana had done earlier. Nevertheless, I quickly jumped into a pedal boat and began pedaling as fast as I could to get to him.

As I got closer, I could see that he was stranded on a reef. He had been caught in an area of broken-glass sharpness on the reef's surface. Thankfully, I had on reef shoes and was able to walk out to get him. By now he had started to cry because he had been stranded for so long. I held him closely, comforting him as I did everything I could to lift him and carry him to the pedal boat.

Once in the boat, good spirit that he was, Matt started laughing as he replayed the incident moment by moment, describing how many times he had frantically waved at me for help—only to watch me simply wave back and then drop my head back into my book. I had thought he was letting me know he was OK, when in reality, he was sending panic signals.

When I heard his perspective, I had to laugh, too. Again, we both got tickled—and the tickle soon turned into a side splitter.

14

Goa: Riots

Months passed quickly, and before we knew it, Christopher was returning for a summer visit. As the time of Christopher's arrival approached, Matt became more and more excited. And once Christopher was back, Matt was a different child. The trauma of Christopher's leaving seemed softened by his return.

We spent the early part of the summer in Dubai, and to escape the 120-degree heat, we took a family vacation to India in early July. Michael had a few days of business in Bombay (now Mumbai) and thought it would be a nice way to kill two birds with one stone.

We landed in Bombay late at night, and as we disembarked, a flight attendant passed out handfuls of hard candies to each passenger. The boys were ecstatic. I declined, not understanding her gesture until we were outside the airport. Once outside, we were bombarded by beggar children, many of whom were disfigured. Matt went into a tailspin, hollering, "Mom! Do something! Mom, you have to do something!"

By now he was eleven, and in the mind of a young one, parents are supposed to be able to do everything. My heart sank as I witnessed his response to the suffering and pain of the Indian children. *If only I could do something*, I thought to myself. "Give them your candy," I said.

I then watched as he lovingly handed out one or two pieces of candy one child at a time, until it was all gone. As he watched them claw the candy from his extended hand, he studied their faces.

52

I know he was overwhelmed, but from that moment on, he held a compassion for fellow humans that many would not be able to imagine. I felt blessed to witness this experience.

We spent two days in Bombay, and then we took the long taxi ride to Goa, where just outside the city, we were halted by a large group of protesters who had formed a roadblock made of large stones. Before we knew it, our taxi was surrounded. The driver rolled down the window, speaking in a tongue unknown to us, and after a few nods and bobs of the head, we were allowed to pass through.

Immediately, I asked him what had just happened. Calmly, he said, "Madam, the protesters are angry about having to speak English in their schools and are fighting for teaching the children in their native dialect. They plan to do more harmful things if they are not heard, so it is advisable for you to remain on the grounds of Fort Aguada once we arrive."

Fort Aguada and its lighthouse constitute a well-preserved seventeenth century Portuguese fort in Goa on the Sinquerim Beach overlooking the Arabian Sea. The place was originally constructed to host the prestigious Association of Southeast Asian Nations meeting (ASEAN Summit), and it was transformed into a resort once the summit concluded.

The living quarters were "huts," each a separate building generously spaced on a hillside so that none was visible to the others. All were delicately situated in the lush tropical environment, each with its own natural flora and landscaping. The huts all had thatched roofs, porches with rockers, rough wood floors, and walls made of claylike material with windows. Ceiling fans were a staple in each room and on the porches, but there was no air conditioning, no phone, and no television.

Our hut had two bedrooms, a full-sized bathroom, and a living room. We had no kitchen amenities—not even a coffee pot. All meals were eaten down the hillside, near the pool in an outdoor restaurant-bar area that looked like a giant gazebo.

It seemed that the moment we arrived, the sky opened up, and the rains did not cease. Unbeknownst to us before leaving for Goa, it was the height of the monsoon season there—and we were stuck inside. After three days, our tiny hut became claustrophobic for the four of us sojourners. So during breaks in the torrential rain, the boys enjoyed skateboarding down all the hills—at least until one day when we met two US military pilots who had flown the US ambassador from Pakistan to India and were staying at the resort with us.

They alerted us to the fact that the riot we had encountered had been very real and should be taken seriously. They also let us know there was no way out of there as long as the roads remained blocked. One of them smiled and said, "Boys, as long as we are here, we could fly you out if you got hurt—broke an arm or leg—on those skateboards. But once we're gone, the likelihood of you getting any help is nil."

That was all it took for Matthew and Christopher to put the skateboards away without a single complaint. In fact, they became quite happy to play volleyball in the swimming pool in the monsoon rains, as long as there was no thunder. But between the rains and the riots, we became virtual captives at the resort. There was absolutely nothing we could do about it either, so the four of us learned how to live in the rain, interact with others in the same situation, and make the best of it.

One day I was sitting on my porch during another downpour, reading the *International Herald Tribune*. The newspaper was at least four days old by the time it arrived at the resort, but I didn't care. I needed something new to read. My 500-page Nelson DeMille book was long finished.

By now, we were approaching two weeks in this "paradise." I scoured the front page and then opened the paper. My eye caught a tiny paragraph at the bottom of the third page's left-hand corner, near the fold. It read, "United States mobilizes the USS Kennedy for war games in the Middle East."

My heart raced, and I called for Michael and read the short paragraph aloud to him. He looked at me quizzically. Given my job responsibilities at the bank, I had been keeping a close eye on the "big picture" of events in my nine-country region and on the political rhetoric that had been flying about for months. I told Michael I didn't have a good feeling about this; something was up. I suggested we cut this nirvana short and start trying to get back to Dubai.

Fortunately, the riots stopped long enough for us to get to Bombay, and by July 30, we were back in Dubai. We never made it into the town of Goa or to the beaches.

15

Back in Dubai: Seeds of War

On the morning of August 2, 1990, I walked into the bank early as usual—only to find my colleague Jean-Pierre running across the bank lobby in his pajamas, hands in the air, fists shaking, and shouting in his heavy Lebanese-French accent, "Oh, Meendy, they did it! They did it!"

"Did what?" I asked. He was in such a tizzy, he didn't hear me. I was shocked by the fact that he was at the bank early—he usually arrived at 11:30 a.m.—let alone in his pajamas.

I followed him across the lobby, trying to understand what was going on. "Who did what? What is going on?" I asked loudly.

"They did it! They did it!" is all he kept shouting.

Finally, I got in front of him, just outside of the dealing room, where I could see all the traders in their undershirts or pajama tops. I shouted, "WHAT THE HELL HAS HAPPENED?"

"They did it! Iraq invaded Kuwait!" Jean-Pierre finally said. "I got a call earlier this morning from one of my private banking clients, who alerted me to protect his wealth."

"Holy shit," I sighed, as I gently dropped into a chair next to one of the traders. Before my eyes, I watched monies move, funds flow, and dealers protect positions before the rest of the world had any clue what was happening.

In the chaos, I realized I had corporate clients in Kuwait and had to jump into action myself. I grabbed Jonathan—the general manager of the bank—and together, we contacted my major Fortune 500 multinational oil company client to get a direct assessment of what was going on. In the background, we could hear gunfire, bombing, and screaming—the situation was clearly serious. I then contacted as many other clients as I could before communication lines went dead.

In less than an hour, we provided London with as accurate a risk assessment as possible. It seemed I was the only bank employee in the Middle East with significant credit exposure in Kuwait, and since it was secured by oil and gas revenues, I did not get overly concerned.

Word of the invasion was getting around through the expatriate multinational business community by word of mouth, but nothing was official. The bank had Reuters communications, but beyond that, nothing but a direct phone call into Kuwait was available—and only if phone lines had not been destroyed. I was concerned about how to communicate this to the boys, so I called Michael and asked him to meet me for a very late lunch.

On August 3, the board members of the American Business Council were debriefed by the US Consulate. We were directed to not gather in large groups, to take different routes to work each day, and to know what and how to communicate to other Americans if executing the formal evacuation plan should become necessary. Fortunately, many expatriate wives and children were out of the country for the summer holiday.

Late in the evening of August 7, I got a phone call at home from an "economics officer" at the US Consulate—someone who I now know was CIA—asking what I thought about the prospect of the US government issuing an evacuation notice. In the background, I could hear what sounded like activity on a military base.

Personally, I felt confident in the intelligence work I had done as part of my job at the bank, and I believed I had as good a grip on the area's events as anyone. I told him I believed an evacuation order would be OK as long as it was done in such a way as not to cause panic. I mentioned that Michael and I were leaving for the airport as soon as I got off the phone to get the boys on a plane to the United States that night.

"You are?" he questioned, with an odd tone in his voice.

"Yes," I said firmly, "I do not need the United States government to tell me how serious the situation is over here. The USS Kennedy is nowhere nearby, and if biological or chemical warfare should begin, we are downwind sitting ducks. Likewise, should our desalination plant be tampered with or should a bomb explode on the airport runway, there would be no flights in or out.

"And from a different security viewpoint, the World Trade Centre is the tallest building in the Middle East and would be an easy target. If Saddam crosses the border into Saudi in an attempt to overtake Mecca—even if it's the slightest gesture—only God knows how bad things could become.

"So again, if you are seriously asking my opinion, I suggest something low-key. Many families are out of the country anyway."

He then told me that the Egyptians had sent fighter jets our way and that he had just arrived at a clandestine locale in the desert to greet them.

In the wee hours of August 9, Michael and I were awakened by the ringing of the telephone. It was Michael's company, mandating that we evacuate per US government instructions. We were directed to pack up our household goods and ship them to Singapore. Michael was to get any valuable paperwork from the office and secure it in case the worst were to occur. I phoned Ralph, my immediate supervisor, to alert him to the news; he was shocked that the British government had not issued evacuation notices.

He asked that I come in as usual but not mention that I had been asked to evacuate by my government, for that in itself might create panic among others in the bank. However, I was free to speak with my immediate colleagues, as my workload had to be transferred. By 3:00 p.m. I had left the bank, not knowing whether I would ever see any of my fellow employees again. I said good-bye just as I did every day.

I was dazed when I pulled up to our now completely empty house, with all our household goods crated in the front yard, waiting to be loaded on a truck. Only a few hours prior, everything had been pristinely in its place. Michael informed me that we had a KLM flight departing the next morning at 2:00 a.m. and that we needed to get to the airport very early.

We made it to the airport early, but there were so many evacuees that we could not get out on KLM. Fortunately, with full-fare first-class tickets, we were able to shift to Lufthansa. Our layover was in Frankfurt, where we were delayed nearly eight hours to accommodate the onslaught of arriving US military aircraft and cargo planes.

The area off the primary tarmac was full of private Saudi, Jordanian, Kuwaiti, and other Middle Eastern royal family jets that were now parked in the safety of Europe. This was the beginning of what would become known as Desert Shield and then Desert Storm.

16

Baton Rouge: Politics, Religion, and Poetry

Safely back in the United States, we were happily reunited with Matthew at my parents' house, outside Houston. Christopher remained in Florida with his mother.

It took our bodies two or three days to start to relax. At the end of the week, Michael flew to Colorado to work, while Matt and I stayed in Texas awaiting our next steps. Our lives and world had just been turned upside down, and we were eager to get resettled. School would be starting in a few weeks, and Matt definitely needed to be settled before the first day. He seemed to have been doing better in Dubai, but with this monkey wrench of having to evacuate, I had no idea what to anticipate next.

The bank was prepared to relocate me to Singapore until things blew over in the Middle East, but Michael's company was not willing to have him based there, even temporarily. So here I was again—same song, different verse: I could follow my desires—medical school, master's degree, professional career—and break up the family, or I could put it all on hold again for the sake of us all being together. Much to my dismay, I realized that I epitomized the "trailing spouse."

I wasn't privy to the discussions Michael was having with his company, so I was mortified to learn that we were being transferred to Baton Rouge, Louisiana. What a professional setback for me! Louisiana law is under the Napoleonic Code, and the state is the only one of the fifty that has selectively rather than fully adopted the Uniform Commercial Code. I felt I was in the worst third-world country I had ever lived in.

As bad as it appeared, at least we knew where we were going and the next steps we needed to take. Once in Baton Rouge, we lived in a Marriott Residence Inn for months before finding something more permanent. Matt began attending a private Episcopal school—but within two months, he could no longer stand being made fun of and being called a "sand nigger." I was so disappointed that Matt's worldly experiences weren't valued, and I quickly moved him to another private school where there was much less prejudice.

I felt blessed to find a new psychologist, Dr. Taylor, close by to pick up where we had left off with Dr. Schanning months earlier. From a much bigger perspective, it felt like God had made the decision about us leaving Dubai when I could not. At least now, Matt could get the help he needed no matter how long it took. But the conundrum came when I read Dr. Taylor's report:

> *Roberts Apperception Test for Children: Projective Hypothesis—"In describing his drawing, Matt suggested a story of an individual with a great deal of self-denial wanting to **help and heal other persons** and expressing few fears or inadequacies".*

Dr. Taylor explained that interpretation of the Roberts Apperception Test for Children is based on the "projective hypothesis," an assumption that when presented with ambiguous drawings of children and adults in everyday interaction, children will project their characteristic thoughts, concerns, conflicts, and coping styles into the stories they create. During the test, the individual is presented with a series of drawings and is asked to create stories describing what is happening in each situation, what led up to it, and how it will end.

There was no recommendation for residential care, however, and I believed that to be positive.

★ ★ ★

Once Michael and Matt were out of the house each day, I was left with myself and the deep sadness of losing the best professional opportunity I had ever had. I wanted to blame Michael, but I couldn't. If anyone were to blame, it was Saddam Hussein. I was angry that Michael's company had no interest or flexibility in a temporary Singapore move that would accommodate my needs, too.

I had a difficult time with this move, and I felt I had to do something to change the catatonic state I experienced when I focused on what I had lost; the lack of closure I felt with so many clients, colleagues, and friends; and how trapped I felt. Again, if I did what I wanted to do professionally, I would break up the family. Dr. Taylor encouraged me to "take care of myself and my needs," but that concept was so foreign to me that I couldn't understand it at the time.

By now, I had awareness of other women that Michael "kept" on his travel circuit, particularly an Australian. One evening I unintentionally intercepted a phone call from her at our new home. Unusual, I thought, that no matter where we moved, she knew how to reach him. I made it clear to her that I existed, just as I had to the woman in Singapore, but I told this one that I would make it easy for her by adding her to our Christmas card list. Then I handed the receiver to Michael and left the room.

★ ★ ★

Since I was unable to find work comparable to what I had been doing for the past several years, I had to create my own work. I had always heard about Louisiana politics, so I decided to work on Buddy Roemer's gubernatorial reelection campaign as a way to meet others and get a better understanding of the business environment in the area. Roemer lost the primary to David Duke, a known Ku Klux Klan leader, which sent everyone I knew to the support of Edwin Edwards—a known crook! I had asked for a ride—and boy, did I get one!

In the meantime, the Gulf War had stopped, and I took advantage of my recent knowledge of the area coupled with my oil and gas background to start my own consulting company. Although the good ole boys of Louisiana didn't much like dealing with a woman in such a role, they realized that I knew my stuff and could be of great value to them in getting their bids through the reconstruction process in the Middle East.

As a result of this work, I was contacted by the Department of Economic Development of the State of Louisiana to help smaller businesses gain a foothold in international markets. I had fun doing this, but professionally, the work didn't hold a candle to the power of what I had lost. However, I felt blessed to have become connected to the business community at the level I did in such a short time, and I found myself being asked to assist at a legislative level in rewriting older laws that no longer served the highest good of Louisiana businesses. It seemed I truly created my own work as I went.

★ ★ ★

Matt led us to a church, First United Methodist, primarily because his new closest friend, Tad, and Tad's family went there. I was indifferent, but I did make an appointment to meet with the minister, Rev. Chris Andrews. I shared with him my experiences and some of my "aha" moments about the other religious cultures I had lived in. Although my path was that of Christianity, I told him I wasn't sure I bought it the way "they" sold it, and I didn't know if he wanted someone like me in his congregation. With great humility, he smiled, saying, "I am honored to have you as part of this congregation."

Something really started moving in me as I became increasingly restless with the idea of merely accepting what I had been told about religion. I embarked on a journey of finding out for myself. During these months, I had many profound spiritual experiences, and I felt blessed to have Chris Andrews as my spiritual mentor.

At his suggestion, I attended a powerful three-day spiritual retreat known as Cursillo, or The Walk to Emmaus. It was here that I had my first experience of a visitation of someone who had passed away. I had full sensation and knowledge of who it was, I could "see" her in spirit form, and we communicated in a way I had never experienced before. I was deeply shaken when I realized it was on the road to Emmaus where Jesus appeared to others the third day after his death.

Admittedly, this was frightening to me, but I clearly remember Rev. Chris saying, "Mindy, either something very holy is going on with you, or you are just short of a little white jacket. I am 'in the business,' and I have never had such intense experiences."

We both laughed as I said, "Time will tell." He suggested I start journaling about these profound occurrences—and I did.

Matt seemed very happy. It was as though he had finally settled in and was doing well in all facets of his life. He asked for a crucifix for Christmas, and it seemed to stay around his neck all the time. He was industrious, starting his own cottage business: trimming hedges, painting, and mowing lawns. It seemed the trauma of evacuation and all its losses was slowly fading. He played football, soccer, and basketball, and although he often expressed dismay at Michael's absence, he seemed to enjoy being with his friends.

One day when I picked him up from school, he slipped into the backseat just as he had when Christopher lived with us and asked, "Hey, Mom, can I read aloud what I wrote in school today?"

"Yes," I said, "that would be great," as I turned the radio down.

He began:

> *"The night got cold, but the*
> *stories kept us warm. As man*
> *acts out the killing of the masculine*
> *mammoth which shall feed us*
> *for the year. The sharp*
> *pointed stone fiercely pierced the*
> *animal wounding it, or in other*
> *words, preparing it for death.*
> *While following the blood tracks*
> *of the animal which is the*
> *size of life, only fear is*
> *found in both man and animal."*

"Whaddaya think?" he asked.

Floored and awed by the depth of these words coming from a twelve-year-old, I responded with, "I like it; where did you copy it from?"

With great frustration, he insisted that he had not copied it. He went on to say that he was perplexed about what title to give it. With the innocence of the child he was, he softly asked again, "Mom, what do you think?"

I suggested he stick it on the refrigerator so it would be in front of him and so that when he felt inspired, he could simply write the title on it.

"OK," he agreed proudly, "I'll do that."

I felt terrible that I had accused him of copying it.

A couple of days later, I noticed that the word "Fear" had been written at the top of the poem on the refrigerator. I stood back, shaking my head at the intelligence and wisdom of his words. His passion for the written word exploded, and like me, he began keeping journals.

Fekman

Fear

The night got cold, but the stories kept us warm. As man acts out the killing of the masculin mammoth which shall feed us for the year. The sharp pointed stone fiercly pierced the animal wounding it, or in other words preparing it for death. While following the blood tracks of the animal which is the size of life, only fear is found in both man & animal.

In early 1992, Michael came home again with news of yet another transfer. It seemed he had become his company's "cleanup" man domestically for regions that were not performing optimally. I felt sucker punched. How much could one company possibly ask of a family that had been through what we had? I was just getting comfortable where I was, and under no circumstances was I moving Matt again.

Michael decided to accept the position and move to California. Matt and I could follow when school was out that June, assuming the company still wanted Michael on the West Coast. Dear God, what was going on? These moves were no longer fun. They had become ridiculous.

During the six months that Michael was stationed in California, he came back to see us in Louisiana twice. In June, when school was out, Matt and I reluctantly left the world we had recently come to love. Both of us had found connection and purpose, only to lose it again.

17

Southern California: Earthquakes

I didn't know how I felt about this move. I was still connected to my spiritual mentor, but only through written letters. Much was going on inside me: my abilities to "see" things that weren't there—to sense, feel, and know things—seemed just to have dropped into my being from the ethers and were now an everyday occurrence.

Just before leaving Baton Rouge, I had a very real dream that Michael and Matthew were abruptly taken away from me—like death. The pain I felt penetrated to my core, becoming unbearable when—in what seemed like a nanosecond—a powerful voice assured me all would be OK and they would not be hurt. I felt comforted but seriously shaken by this experience. Was this a foreshadowing or just a bad lucid dream?

We found a church to attend—I longed for a place to belong— but the vibes just weren't there. Frequently that summer, we made our way into Los Angeles to watch the Dodgers, Michael and Matt's favorite baseball team. But for the most part, I felt in total limbo. There was no indication from Michael's company how long we might be in Fullerton.

★ ★ ★

With no warning and out of a deep sleep, I made an abrupt face-plant onto the floor at 4:47 a.m. the morning of June 28, 1992. My first thought was that Michael had forcefully kicked me out of bed for some reason. But as I attempted to stand up, I could see him on the other side of the bed trying to stand up as well. Loudly, he yelled, "Earthquake!"

The floor beneath us was rolling. One step and a knee would be under our chin; the next, the floor would be so far away that our feet didn't touch the ground. Both in our birthday suits, we made our way through the rolling-wave motions to a pile of dirty clothes at the foot of the bed, covered our bodies, and frantically made our way to Matt's room. He was sound asleep, dead center in his king-sized bed. Michael scooped him up, doing his best not to fall down as we scurried from the bottom floor up to street level. Climbing the stairs was nearly impossible.

Once on the living-dining level of our home, we saw the chandelier swinging almost 180 degrees across the dining table. Kitchen cabinet doors were flung open; contents were broken on the counter and floor; and canned goods, flour, sugar, and glasses from the bar shelves were strewn and shattered all over the place.

No warning, no preparedness, and no escape—Mother Earth had just opened up and graced us with the experience of a 7.3-magnitude earthquake, with the epicenter in the nearby Landers area of California. Up to that point, we had believed evacuating Dubai was traumatic!

After our unsettling introduction to California, Matt and I decided to goof off for the remainder of the summer. We did our best to make the most of it, not knowing if we would be there long enough for him to start school and for me to look for work.

We met one group of friends from Dubai in Jackson Hole, Wyoming, for a week, and then we moseyed on over to Oregon to visit another family for a week. Michael was asked to be the best man in the wedding of Marty's former spouse, which was being held in Houston that summer. Matt went to Texas with Michael to stay with my parents for a visit, while Marty came to California to spend time with me.

I had been by Marty's side, a confidante of sorts, over the past decade. Her former spouse had had an affair with another friend of ours while we were in Singapore, and while the other couple had healed their relationship, Marty and her husband had not. Marty had stayed in denial and continued to wear her wedding ring all this time. She had taken her oath literally, and in her mind, she was still married until death they did part.

Marty and I guessed the time when her former husband would be stating his vows to his new wife. I held Marty as she wept and wept, finally removing the tri-band golden ring from her left finger.

The summer quickly came to a close, and with no word from Michael's company, we had no choice but to look for a new school for Matt. Of all the places we had lived, this location was the most disturbing to me. The city was so large! Gangs were rampant, and drive-by shootings occurred daily. I was now faced with finding a good school where my fragile child could succeed and be safe.

It took a while, but we decided on Fairmont, a private school in Anaheim that was about a thirty-minute drive away. The school was a melting pot of nationalities, which was exactly the kind of environment Matt felt most comfortable in.

Each day, I drove Matt to school and picked him up. I had deep conversations with him about gangs, making him aware that most of the gang members were straight-A students of Asian descent—not what one would expect. Matt excelled in school and in football and seemed to be much happier in his new world than I was in mine.

Our drives to and from school gave us lots of time to be together and talk. His compassion for the homeless on the streets took me back to our trip to India, so he and I decided we would keep food in the car every day so we could stop and give it out. Together we went to the grocery store and got canned foods with pull tabs, juice boxes, and plastic utensils—all of which we put in bags and passed out en route to or from school. Over time, we decided to add home-cooked leftovers, which he would place each night into plastic disposable containers and pack into bags for the next morning's ride.

One morning, about a mile away from school, we saw the yellow outline of a body on the sidewalk: another soul lost to the violence of the gangs. A cold silence passed through the car as both of us realized what had happened. That afternoon, when I picked Matt up from school, he told me that a girl from his school had been walking to McDonald's at lunch and had been shot. Fortunately, she had been carrying her books close to her chest, so the bullet did not make it into her body. I hated this place with a passion.

Each day, when I returned home from taking Matt to school, I was left with myself and my thoughts. My spiritual gifts and abilities continued to grow, but what bothered me was the distance I felt from Michael. After all, I had been bounced all over the planet following his career, so why did I feel he didn't he even SEE me? I longed to be noticed by him, but that's about where it stayed—in the realm of longing.

One evening in early October, Michael came home with the news that his company was ready to transfer us. They had several possibilities available for us, and since I had been the one who had lost the most professionally as a result of our recent moves, I was to be a large factor in the decision about where we were to go next.

In the process, I asked that the three of us write down what we wanted in a new place to live. We nixed Europe, because that would place Matt back in the United States his senior year of school. We also decided not to go back to places we had previously lived—like Boulder and Baton Rouge. Everyone wanted outdoors. I wanted the ocean; Matt and Michael wanted mountains. I wanted some semblance of a profession again. Matt wanted fishing. In the end, the location we selected was Charlotte, North Carolina. We were to leave immediately after Matt's last school event, a Halloween party.

At 10:00 p.m. October 30, Michael and I picked up Matt from the school Halloween party. My heart bled for him; he had straight As, genuinely felt accepted by his peers, and was visible like never before. During his last football game the day before, he had made the winning touchdown, and all the team members had signed the game ball to give Matt, knowing he would be leaving California after the party.

Much to our surprise, when we pulled up to the school, there were police cars everywhere. We learned that several gunmen and their Asian gang members had raided the gym, holding the Halloween partygoers in sheer fright.

In a panic, Michael and I ran inside to find our child. He was looking for us as frantically as we were looking for him. We clutched one another tightly as he said further good-byes to his friends, now connected to them even more closely by this horrific experience.

None of us could sleep on the red-eye flight to Charlotte. Matt needed to talk, and I needed to listen to him as he gave me the play-by-play, moment-by-moment account of what had happened in the gym his last night in California. My body shook as I thought of what could have been, with thanks and blessings for how things had turned out. I could only imagine the fear pulsating through my young eighth grader, reciting in my mind his own written words: *"While following the blood tracks of the animal which is the size of life, only fear is found in both man and animal."*

We landed in Charlotte at 5:00 a.m., holding hands, wide awake.

18

Charlotte: Something Major Changes

It was late August 1993, and we were finally settled in our new home in South Charlotte—we even had pictures on the walls. Strange, but hanging pictures was how I gauged the length of time we'd probably be in a location.

We had 1.25 acres of land in the city and a dream home made of wood and stone. We had two beautiful, handmade wood-burning stone fireplaces; visibility to the outdoors from every room; and a covered back porch where Michael and I sat each evening to enjoy a beer after work, watching the kids play football and the dogs play chase. Life seemed to be settling down after evacuating from the Middle East, living like nomads for months, relocating to Baton Rouge and then Fullerton in less than eighteen months—and experiencing a 7.3-magnitude earthquake during our four-months' residence in the latter.

In September, I was to begin a job as a financial analyst at First Union, a regional bank headquartered in Charlotte. My talents were much greater than what this job required, but unfortunately, the bank was too small to offer much else. The job was better than flipping burgers at McDonald's, but professionally, it was a step so far backward that it upset me.

The first year in Charlotte, Matt attended Providence Day School. It was the only school that allowed him to transfer his early-semester "A" in chemistry, a ninth-grade course in Charlotte but an eighth-grade course at his previous private school in Anaheim.

I understood what it felt like from an adult perspective to continually move and have to make new social contacts, learn the ropes of a new city, look for new employment, and often go backward to start life all over again. Unlike Michael, who maintained continuity of contacts and relationships through his work colleagues, the children and I had no such continuity. I could only imagine what it was like for Matt at such a young, pivotal age to have to uproot his life and friends to begin anew so many times.

These moves had seemed more bearable for him when Christopher was still with us. Continually moving and being uprooted was an experience the two of them had shared, each one being the only constant for the other in the equation.

Although Michael was "there," he was always either travelling or noticeably distant emotionally—another element of our lives that Matt and I shared.

★ ★ ★

There is something about being a mother that simply defies explanation. In the middle of the night about three months after settling into our new home, I awakened abruptly, not understanding why. As I lay quietly in bed, I heard a faint, muffled, rhythmic beat, but I couldn't determine where it was coming from. Was it in my head? Had I just awakened from a dream? What was it?

Suddenly, something forced me up and out of bed. I made my way in the darkness to the bedroom door and opened it, and through the shadows, I saw Matt sprawled out on the hallway floor about five or six feet from my doorway, beating the floor with one hand. He was having a severe asthma attack.

I ran to him and picked him up, trying to calm him. But I could tell he was not breathing. I screamed for Michael to come and hold him while I ran to the kitchen to get the epinephrine—which he had to have if he were to have a chance to live. His breath was virtually gone.

I could *not* lose it. I had to maintain composure to get the proper dosage of medicine in the syringe to help him; otherwise, I could kill him. Thank God I had been taught what to do in a situation like this! There was no time for second-guessing, only calmness and deep love. I injected him once and waited to see how his body would respond. Some breath came back, but after fifteen minutes, I had to inject him again. More breath came back.

I took him from Michael's arms and held him in my arms, cradling him, creating a calming space to keep him from panicking further. Slowly, Matt's breath came back to a deep, normal volume. He wanted to go back to sleep, so I sat up with him the rest of the night to make sure he kept breathing.

★ ★ ★

On the eve of August 26, I hired a limousine and invited two newly met neighborhood couples to join us for a night of country-and-western dancing and a champagne celebration at a local nightclub, a surprise in honor of Michael's forty-fourth birthday. Matt spent the night with a friend in the neighborhood.

The limo brought us back to our house around midnight. We said our good-byes and the neighbors walked home. Michael was fumbling around, trying to get in the back door when I felt an urge to go to the front of the house. I walked around the house, and as I approached the front steps, I fell down on them, crying out, "Something is wrong with Matt! Something is wrong, and I don't know what it is!"

I could not stop crying; the feeling I had in my body was like none I had ever felt before. It was indescribable, no matter how much

I tried to relate it to something familiar. I felt something serious had occurred—or was happening now. I just had no clue what it was.

Michael had made it into the house by now and opened the front door to find me vomiting violently. My entire body writhed and was in such deep spasm that all I could do was cry out that something was wrong with Matt. "We have to help him!" I screamed. "My Matt—something is wrong—what is it?"

My limp body was sprawled over the front steps. "Matt's fine," Michael said, blowing me off as having had too much to drink. "I think you just had a little too much fun."

But we both knew better.

19

Get Thee Behind Me, Satan!

The acrid smell of sulfur emanated from Matt's room one Saturday afternoon while I was vacuuming the hallway. Immediately, I stepped in, only to back out quickly, turning to run and get my Bible in the next room. In the hallway on my way back to Matt's room, I felt I met the devil face-to-face at the doorway to my son's room and instantly began the battle for my child.

Neither Matt nor Michael was home when I went against the biggest, baddest energy-being I had ever experienced. But no matter the size, there was no presence too big for this mother! I entered the room shouting, "Satan! Get thee behind me!" I opened windows, stripped the bed, flipped the mattress, took all towels and sheets out of the closet, opened drawers, and smudged clothes—completely turning his room and the adjoining bathroom upside down.

During my frenzy, something wrapped in plastic and hidden among the towels fell onto the floor. Intuitively, I put the packet in my pocket to be dealt with later.

My spiritual gifts had continued to develop, seemingly daily. I was continually awakened by "knowings," and while I did not consciously know what I was doing with this horrific presence, something inside me got me through the ordeal with ease, grace, and no fear.

These days, Matt seemed to be spinning out of control. Michael was absent even when physically present, and my struggle to keep our family together was like trying to hold water in my hands. Matt's behavior became so difficult that we thought removing him from his current situation would be helpful. So in the fall of 1993, we enrolled him at Hargrave Military Academy in Chatham, Virginia.

I cried and cried, sensing that he felt we were abandoning him— but what more could we do? I was the one trying so hard to help, to understand what was happening, while Michael literally did nothing. Matt frequently ran away and would be gone for days. I became a basket case, driving around looking for him, panicked that something had happened to him—while Michael seemed unfazed. He wouldn't even leave the house to look for Matt.

Officer Bill, our neighborhood policeman, and Joe, our youth minister, helped me look for Matt; they would also look for him on their own. I had been counseled by both a psychiatrist and a psychologist to stop handling everything—to take a backseat and let Michael step up to the plate in his child's life. But Michael wouldn't budge.

Before going to Hargrave, Matt admitted to "trying" drugs, which was another reason in my mind to remove him from Charlotte. We were pretty sure that the "something" I had found in Matt's closet wrapped in plastic was drugs.

In the spring of 1994, with Matt still at Hargrave, Michael and I were sitting in bed one morning, drinking our first cup of coffee. Michael looked at me and said, "I don't know if I want to be married to you anymore. I'll let you know." Jokingly, I replied, "Well, I would hope you would!"

Michael wanted to take a job in China, to which I emphatically said, "No!" He seemed very distant and aloof. I didn't say anything more, as I seriously believed him to be joking.

But as the days passed, I realized he was not joking. Michael's behavior became unusual. He would leave for days with no word about where he was or what he was doing. He told me he was taking a job in China but failed to do anything about it or proceed with not being married to me anymore. It was crazy-making!

Then, that fall, Matt went AWOL from Hargrave. When I got the phone call, the commanding officer told me they had found him several miles from the school "walking to Charlotte." He had told them that his mother was all alone and that all he was doing was going home to her. My heart hurt so badly when I heard this.

Hours later I got to the school to pick him up. We went through the paperwork and process for withdrawal, and as we made our way back to the car, we stood in the courtyard holding each other, sobbing.

★ ★ ★

I had been advised by Officer Bill that it was not a good idea for Matt to come back to Charlotte. The guys he had been hanging out with previously were being watched as potential gang members and druggies. I freaked, remembering how horrible the gangs were in California, and I asked my parents if Matt could live with them in Texas and go to school there, believing it would be safer for him. They were available to help in any way they could.

I discussed this option with Matt, and while he agreed to do it, something still seemed awry.

20

The Warning

One afternoon early in December 1994, while buried deep in a project with a deadline the next day, I received a phone call from my parents. I answered, "Hello," but before my next breath, my mother frantically said, "Mindy, come quickly! Something is wrong with Matt. He's OK, but there's been an incident with a gun! We're at the hospital in Beaumont."

My heart raced. I panicked, quickly asking questions. But she simply said, "Just get here as fast as you can."

I arrived at St. Elizabeth's Hospital in Beaumont late that evening and was told I could not see Matt until the next morning. Through tears, I begged the nurse to let me see my son. "He's my only child," I pleaded, "and he needs me. Please let me see him." She let me in for a little while, but Matt's doctor had medicated him, and he was fast asleep. As I hugged and kissed him, his big brown eyes opened slightly and he smiled at me, squeezing my hand before drifting back into sleep.

I went downstairs to the waiting room to find my parents. "What in the world happened today?" I implored, hoping to get the complete story rather than the pieces I had received en route. They told me Matt had come home from school seemingly loaded on what they believed to be pot. He seemed angry and confused. He shouted that he wasn't good enough, and while standing in front of my father's chair, Matt pulled out a pistol and put it to his temple.

My mother entered the room from the kitchen with a load of laundry that she dropped on the floor when she realized what she was witnessing. She and my father both kept talking to Matt, encouraging him to take the gun away from his head and put it down. Eventually, he dropped the gun in my father's lap and ran into the bedroom, throwing himself on the bed and crying hysterically. My mother did what she could to console him, but her efforts were to no avail. They got him in the car and rushed him to the emergency room in Beaumont.

While waiting, they rehashed the incident over and over. My mother said to my father, "Thank God that gun wasn't loaded!" At which time my father reached into his pocket, pulled out a clinched fist, and opened his hand to reveal a single .22-caliber bullet shining in his palm—the one the gun had held.

While retelling the story to me, he reached into his pocket and pulled out the same bullet. There were no words to describe my feelings. For now, Matt was safely sleeping upstairs.

★ ★ ★

Before leaving North Carolina, I had called Michael's company alerting them to the emergency and asking for their assistance in finding him in China. I had no other way to locate him. Not long after I left the hospital with my parents, we received a phone call from Michael letting us know he should be in Texas in one-and-a-half to two days. In the meantime, I would be there with Matt and the doctor.

Matt was under pretty tight ropes. I could not stroll in and out at will—only during certain hours and for very short visits. My first appointment was with Matt's doctor, Paul Baker. I did my best to relay the events of our lives up to this moment. I also contacted every counselor, psychologist, or psychiatrist we had previously worked with to ask that they provide their insights to Dr. Baker so he could do an accurate assessment of the situation, given this latest event. He let me know in no uncertain terms the seriousness of what we were facing, and he seemed anxious to speak with Michael to round out his assessment.

Michael arrived the third day, angry that I had contacted his company to find him. Somewhat blowing him off, I snidely said, "I would think a father would want to be with his child if his child had attempted suicide and were hospitalized." Dr. Baker was quick to have Michael come to his office, directing me to sit tight until he needed me. Michael saw Matt, but not before seeing Dr. Baker.

That evening when Michael was leaving, he let me know he was staying near the airport in Houston at Marty's and would be driving back and forth from there to the hospital. Odd, I thought, that he didn't want to be closer to Matt—and even odder when he had to request that our morning appointments not be too early because he had a two-hour drive!

After a couple of days with Michael, Dr. Baker asked the two of us to come to his office. He reiterated the seriousness of the situation, indicated that Matt had admitted to greater drug usage than we knew about, and succinctly stated that the root of the problem was that the child needed his father. He lectured us about what we needed to do to make a safe home environment for Matt, and he then again emphasized that Matt needed Michael to be present and emotionally available.

Then Dr. Baker asked each of us, "Given all you have heard, which one of you is going to take this child when I release him from the hospital tomorrow?"

Michael responded immediately, saying he just couldn't do it because he was working in China. I said I could do it because I loved Matt and I wanted to help him. In deep frustration, Dr. Baker said, "Did neither of you hear what I just said about this child seriously needing his father? I want the two of you to leave, discuss this between yourselves, and be back in this office in one hour. Do you understand?" I left feeling like a seriously scolded schoolkid.

We walked across the street to a restaurant and ordered a Coke. Michael had nothing to say; he just sat there, vacant. I opened the conversation by repeating what Dr. Baker had said. Michael vehemently restated there was absolutely no way he could take Matt. He had a job in China, and he didn't know what he would possibly do with Matt there. He would not even listen to suggestions about possible solutions.

After thirty minutes of beating my head against a wall, I got up and walked back to Dr. Baker's office. Michael followed sheepishly.

Once inside, Dr. Baker motioned for us to sit down. Immediately, he asked, "So, what is your decision? Who will be taking Matt when I release him?" Silence overcame the room. I had been counseled enough by other psychologists to know that I had to be quiet and let Michael step up. Dr. Baker looked us up and down, saying nothing, patiently awaiting the first sound to break the silence.

Deep inside, I held hope that Michael would have a change of heart. But no! The first utterance came from Michael, who simply stated, "I cannot take him. I have a job in China."

Dr. Baker looked at Michael and said, "You are immediately excused from the room. There is nothing for you to do here; please leave."

Dr. Baker looked at me, shaking his head in disgust. He said in all his years of practice, he had not seen anyone as *alexithymic* (having no emotional awareness of self or others) as Michael. Dr. Baker peered over his half-glasses and locked eyes with me, leaning toward me over his desk. He told me I was dealing with a situation similar to that of an inner-city black mother who has male children with fathers who are in absentia.

"Your chances of success with this child are slim to none," he said. "He admits to drug usage, which I predict will worsen, not get better. Again, your chances with him are minimal. I wish I had better news for you, but I don't. When I said Matt needed his father,

I meant it. You are not his father, and you will never be. The child needs his father, and you cannot possibly fill both roles. Therefore, accept before you leave my office that your chances of helping this child are nil."

Stunned and in shock, all I could say was, "The more you tell me I can't, the more I am motivated to prove you wrong."

Smiling at me, he said, "You're admirable. But you have a long, difficult road ahead of you. Now let's talk about putting a plan together for you and Matt to get out of here."

21

Tough Love

Once we were back in Charlotte, Matt started a day-patient program at a rehabilitation facility called Amethyst. I was able to drop him off on my way to work and pick him up on my way home. By this time, Michael and I had split, our house had been sold—and true to form, Michael was nowhere to be found. He had removed everything he wanted earlier and had left all loose ends and the closing to me.

Christmas was upon us, and it could not have occurred at a worse time in our lives. Sadly, on Christmas Eve, Matt and I moved into an apartment not far away. We did all we could to make the most of our situation, but I must admit, it was pretty abysmal. Boxes were stacked floor-to-ceiling in the apartment. Matt screamed out, "This is not Christmas!" I agreed with him and did all I could to be with him, talk to him, and connect with him during this horrible twenty-four-hour period.

I worked frantically around the clock to get the apartment whipped into shape and as much like a home as possible. I asked Matt to fix his room the way he wanted it, which gave him something to focus on for a couple of days. There was no rush to find another school for him to attend. The most important thing was continuing his outpatient care for as long as his counselors believed he needed it.

I started attending counseling sessions and learning about drugs, family dynamics, tough love, and adult children of alcoholics—anything that could help me understand what I was dealing with. It's strange how many of us live with blinders on until something serious or very painful shows up in our lives. I now had a better understanding of what it meant to have the "scales fall from my eyes."

Everything seemed to be going smoothly until one day in mid-January when I picked Matt up from Amethyst. We were almost home when he got really mad about what he was doing. He said he didn't want to do it anymore, and at a red light, he jumped out of the car. He ran off into the darkness so fast I had no idea where he went. I had been taught not to go after him. So reluctantly, I drove on home and did my best to keep going. I halfway expected him to come home, but he did not.

This behavioral pattern continued for several months. I finally told him that he had a loving, warm home and a place to live and that if he chose not to live there and abide by the rules, he could continue living on the streets. Then one day in May, I came home to find a note from the Department of Social Services taped to my door. Matt had turned me in for child abuse! The social worker came out, interviewed me, and closed the case.

Each day, driving to work, I would see school children getting on the bus. Often, I had no idea where my child was—or whether he was dead or alive. My heart ached so badly for my son; I longed for us to live more normally. I would end up crying so hard that all my makeup would run down my face. I despised starting my day this way, but try as I might, I could not hide the depth of pain I was carrying.

Once I got to my parking lot at work, I'd try to hide until I could slip into the closest bathroom to clean myself up before beginning my day's work. Inside, I felt empty, and by now, I had placed my heart on a shelf because the pain was so great I couldn't function any other way.

I alerted all of my colleagues and superiors to what I was dealing with. Hiding the fact that my son was a runaway, did drugs, and often got into trouble with the police was not my way of handling the truth. Besides, it was no reflection on me. I needed all the help and support I could get, and work was one of the main places I needed it.

Something inside me kept pushing me to discover a different way of living and interacting with my son. Five nights per week for nearly two years, I attended Al-Anon, Nar-Anon, and CODA support group meetings. I also had one-on-one counseling sessions and went to a "tough-love" group. But while much of what I was doing was educational in nature, nothing was helping with the deep pain I felt, nor did it seem to help Matt shift his actions and choices.

It was difficult to push through life when something as serious as my child's drug use and accompanying behaviors were running rampant. I thought I knew God but realized I didn't—until God was all I had. Then I had no choice but to surrender to Him. I pleaded continually with God to take care of and watch over His child, Micah Aaron Matthew Felcman. For God had created him, and God knew where he was and what was happening with him—even when I did not. I asked God to hold me, no matter what happened.

Many nights I cried myself to sleep, often awakened by the blaring sounds of sirens nearby, thinking the emergency could be my Matt. After a few hours and no phone call, I would drift off to sleep again.

22

Energy Medicine

A couple of years later, I completed Leadership Charlotte Class XV, a program with a civic organization that cultivates and trains leaders over a twelve-month period to become actively engaged in the community. As a graduate, I served on various committees each year, depending on my interests and the needs of the organization.

This year, I was part of the selection committee for the upcoming class and was tasked with interviewing potential candidates. My interview partner was the medical director of Presbyterian Hospital, and we used his office to interview prospective candidates over a three-day period.

During these days, we got to know each other fairly well. I shared my frustrations with talk therapy, drugs prescribed by psychiatrists to correct drug problems, and my perceived limitations of certain programs I attended, like "tough love" and the "anon" groups. I kept iterating that there had to be another way. I knew there was something more to dealing with what I was experiencing with my son—I just hadn't discovered it yet.

In response, the medical director referred me to a woman affiliated with the hospital who was "alternative" in her approach to healing. Her name was Christine H., and he said he would have her contact me. She did, and after lengthy discussion, she referred me to another Christine who practiced and taught "energy healing." It was with this woman that the aperture of my mind widened, and when combined with my growing spiritual capabilities, I came to learn that the possibilities for healing were limitless.

I firmly believed in "Ask and ye shall receive." So I was not at all surprised that in my quest for answers, "Christ..." showed up twice! Although I didn't fully understand what I had received, I was open and willing to learn. Thus, I embarked upon a journey foreign to many.

I immersed myself in energy medicine, traveling the globe to study with world-renowned teachers and learning the techniques and skills of indigenous cultures. I exposed myself to quantum physics; vibrational medicine; cutting-edge theories of thought, mind, and consciousness—and the impact of these things on our cellular structure. I learned how unwillingness to change belief systems limits possibilities. I also learned if one is willing to allow the possibility of "what if" or "maybe," the door can be opened for God to come in to expand awareness and to remove limitations.

What I perceived to be "invisible" slowly became visible to me as I continued my studies and hands-on practice. I quickly learned that just because something cannot be seen does not mean it is not there or real. My experiences were finally being validated! Not being able to see electromagnetic waves didn't stop me from tuning into the oldies radio station that I dearly loved or stop me from changing the television station to find my favorite nighttime soap opera.

Before I realized what was happening, interdimensional, multigenerational, and transgenerational healing became part of my everyday experience! I opened myself wide to become a vessel for healing—no matter how different that might look from my original pre-medical studies and desire to become an M.D.

Extraordinarily, as part of my continuing education, the bank supported my interest in healing and my newfound medicine courses. They believed I would be a great contributing member to my community and society at large by sharing what I was learning. I was somewhat flabbergasted but did not hesitate to take advantage of the opportunity to combine my new passion for energy medicine with my existing financial profession.

I now had something to sink my teeth into that I believed could help both Matt and me!

23

The Truth about Michael

During times when Matt was attending support group meetings, working with a sponsor, and demonstrating that he wanted to get his life on track, I shared my newfound healing knowledge and experiences with him—one of which was the sudden onset of a past-life recall I had in which he and I shared a life as medicine men.

In this particular vision, we were working side by side in a cave lit by two burning rags on the end of a stick. There were animal skins covering two very large boulders, flat enough that someone could lie down on them. Hundreds of people—men, women, and children—were lined up outside the cave awaiting their turn to see us for healing. For us, the feeling was one of overwhelming sadness and despondency, for no matter what we did, we were not able to help our tribe. The guilt was forbidding and intense.

This knowledge clearly resonated with Matt, because he sat motionless, listening, absorbing everything I shared and asking questions that seemed triggered by the picture I painted when I spoke of the experience.

When he was in a place to actually "hear" what I was saying, we dialogued frequently. I strongly felt that somehow, our relationship would heal and that we might possibly help others heal, too. We often discussed what a wonderful counselor he would make for others who had experienced life's trials as he had.

But it seemed that these periods of recovery were becoming less frequent, and periods of relapse took up more days on the calendar. The most devastating blow came in 1996, when Matt and I discovered that Michael and Marty had gotten married. The ink was barely dry on our divorce papers.

The emotional impact of this news on Matt was more than his fragile condition could handle. He expressed his rage and anger through vandalism, theft, and more and more drugs. By now I felt completely helpless. Dr. Baker's words kept circling in my head: "The boy needs his father. The chances of success with you are slim to none."

Matt did indeed need his father, and with this latest move, his father was so far removed that it was as if he were dead. Matt's anger at and confusion with Marty was nothing I could satisfactorily explain away either. She had been my best, closest friend for years, and Matt had witnessed that. I had been there for her through so many deeply emotional trials of her life—and this was what I got in return? As they say, the wife is the last to know.

I sensed Matt wanted to protect me in some way, but frankly, both of us were turned upside down, and each of us had to figure out how to handle this news in our own way. Unfortunately, Matt became more and more self-destructive. I tried my best to explain that this situation had absolutely nothing to do with him and that something was out of sorts with his father. None of it made sense, but it certainly hadn't occurred because Matt was a bad person.

Fortunately, in early 1997, Matt voluntarily requested to enter a residential treatment program. I was delighted that he was seeking help, but I almost collapsed under the weight of the $30,000 I had to have in my hands just to get him in the front door. Through God's will, the funds became available for his entrance—but I had no clue where the funds would come from beyond that. I did my best not to concern myself with that burden, as Matt's life and health were foremost.

Matt was in residential care for nine months, and while a lot of good came from his time in the facility, there was even more heartache and disappointment from Michael. The counselors at this facility quickly learned that the behavioral attitudes of Michael's alexithymia were in direct opposition to Matt's deep need for his father. As such, the facility forbade me to pick Matt up at the end of his stay, in order to force Michael to step up as a parent.

Fortunately, Michael showed up to take Matt home. But unfortunately, as a result of his new marriage to Marty, Michael didn't want Matt anywhere around. So he rented an apartment for Matt to live in alone.

My heart ached badly when I learned of this. Matt was trying so hard—and Michael was absolutely out to lunch! Matt ended up getting kicked out of the apartment Michael had gotten for him because he was only eighteen—not old enough to be living there by himself. He ended up sleeping at the pool at the apartment complex until another family took him in.

This cycle continued over the next several years. Matt—who now decided he wanted to be called by his first name, Micah—could do nothing to win his father's affections and emotional support. So he continually resorted to the self-destructive patterns of using drugs. In 2001, Micah overdosed on Tylenol and almost died from the resulting damage to his liver. Medical professionals did not give him long to live and asked that I call in family members.

It was at this time that I learned Michael and Marty had divorced and Michael was being institutionalized with early-onset of Alzheimer's. I returned to the critical-care unit to share this information with Micah, believing it would help him to validate that all the years of his father's emotional absence had had nothing to do with him and everything to do with his father. Unfortunately, my best intentions backfired.

Micah became incensed, insisting that I leave the hospital and leave him alone. He did not want to see me again, and he made a big deal of it to the doctors and nurses who attempted to calm him down. The doctors and nurses asked what I felt was best, but given the circumstances, I had nothing to offer. Legally, Micah was an adult, so there was nothing I could do. I went home.

Micah was released to a mental health facility, and when given the opportunity to make a phone call, he called one of his drug buddies, who picked him up and drove him to a rave in Atlanta.

My body felt crushed. How many times had I called upon and pleaded with God during these near-death relapses? Micah was like a cat with nine lives. How many times could this continue before he didn't make it? Better yet, what about me? This time I was angry and pissed at God and the world. I cried and cried for Jesus, pleading with Him to let me know what He would do. As a mother, what more could I possibly do? How could I relieve the intense pain I felt?

That afternoon, in the quietness of my prayer and meditation, the Presence of Jesus appeared to the right side of my green leather wingback chair. Somewhat in shock, I could not make myself look up at the brilliance of the Presence. Then, it was as though an etheric hand reached out and powerfully lifted my chin to look upward.

As I did, I saw in my mind's eye what Jesus was trying to convey to me: a small, postage stamp–sized photo of Mary over His right shoulder. Somewhat confused, I asked what this meant. The next image I saw was that of a sidewalk divided by a plexiglass partition. I was on one side and Micah was on the other. I could see him and be near him, but I was not to be on his path. Jesus' conveyance of the image of himself was the same. Jesus was at the forefront and Mary was nearby, but she remained on her path and He on his.

The message had nothing to do with love and everything to do with free will. I was grateful for this profound communication, and although it was difficult to continually be faced with these life-or-death challenges, I found a peace inside and again placed Micah in the hands of his true Father.

When Matt decided to be called Micah, it signaled something to me I had learned in my spiritual studies. Often in myth and in the Bible, when someone moves from one spiritual challenge to another or passes certain tests, his or her name changes to carry the vibration of the new path or challenge. For example, Abram changed to Abraham. I sensed the shift in Micah, allowing me to surrender to the interactions between him and his Creator. He always wore a cross—another outward indication to me of a powerful purpose despite my inability to fully grasp what it might be. God was in charge, and my job was to be on the sidelines.

Micah was gone for several weeks after leaving for the rave in Atlanta—and I had no idea where. When he returned, he let me know wanted to visit his father from a place of sobriety and asked if I would go with him. As soon as he felt ready, the two of us traveled to Houston to visit Michael—where we were both brought to tears by what we witnessed. The cause of so many events and actions that we had not been able to make sense of earlier in life immediately became apparent. Unknowingly, we had lived through the early deterioration of Michael's mind.

In retrospect, I thanked God for Marty. God knew I could not have handled both a drug-addicted son and a fifty-two-year-old spouse now institutionalized with full-blown Alzheimer's.

24

Heroin

I fantasized that life would get better for Micah and me now that the cause of Michael's mysterious behavior had been revealed. I hoped that Micah could finally realize that his father had been incapable of giving him the love and affection he had longed for. Difficult as it was, I knew that Michael's Alzheimer's had nothing to do with Micah or me—it was what it was. But this revelation didn't redirect Micah's behavior at all.

Despite Micah's extremely acute intellect, his ability to pull straight As in college, and his gift of the written word, the cycles of relapse and recovery continued. Each time, I encouraged him to pull himself up by the bootstraps, leave yesterday behind, and begin anew in the moment. I did my best to be there for him—to encourage, support, love, and guide him back on track. But one evening in 2004, around dusk, I had my head handed to me on a platter.

I had driven over to his apartment, where I saw a group of people with a lowboy trailer backed up to Micah's door, removing furniture and what appeared to be all of his belongings. Micah was nowhere around. The thought crossed my mind that he was being robbed, but my intuition ruled differently. Jolted and terror stricken, I watched from across the parking lot until the people, truck, and lowboy pulled away.

Once I felt they were far away, I walked cautiously to the door, which was partially ajar. Part of me was fearful I might find Micah inside. I mustered the courage to walk in, feeling deep pain and devastation within myself and sensing it inside the four walls as well. The majority of his furniture, typewriters, books, and most treasured belongings were gone. But what got my attention were the blood tracks, balloon fragments, scorched teaspoon, and small insulin syringes all over the kitchen area near the stove. Oh my God! My heart raced as my mind informed me that I was looking at the remains of a heroin junkie's debris.

Never before had Micah indicated to me his use of heroin. He had shared a lot with me—often much more than I wanted to know—but not this. The physical sight of the interior of what once was a warm, well-tended home hit hard. I knew that if he were alive, the path ahead would be much more difficult than I had ever imagined.

25

The Road to Recovery—Again

About a week after my discovery, I got a phone call from the highway patrol. Micah's car had been found abandoned on the side of the road in South Carolina. I explained to the officer what had happened the previous week, but he told me there had been no sight of Micah. He said the car looked as if it had hit something from underneath—perhaps run up on a curb or median—but there was no gas in it, and it needed to be removed from the highway as soon as possible. He also let me know there was no indication that Micah was in jail, either.

Two friends accompanied me on the three-and-a-half-hour drive to recover Micah's car. Anything that had meaning for him was either in the backseat or in the trunk. But Micah was nowhere to be found, and the interior of the car looked much like that of the kitchen I had discovered a week earlier.

I was numb—I had no clue where my son was or had been. Emotionally, I was about to drop, but I managed to hold myself together to get the car taken care of.

Seven hours later, I arrived home, collapsing in my green chair in a heap and crying uncontrollably. I experienced a greater depth of pain than ever, a place within myself unfamiliar and unknown until then. In this, the greatest state of weakness I had experienced so far, I used every ounce of energy I had to plead with God to take good care of His son, Micah. He knew where Micah was—I did not.

Approximately two weeks later, I received a phone call from Micah wanting to know if I would come for Family Day. Somehow, he had made it back to North Carolina and was in a thirty-day drug-rehab treatment program. Without hesitation, I said I would be there; I could hardly wait to hold and hug him tightly.

He knew I knew about the heroin, and one of the first things he said to me was "Mom, there's nothing out there that I couldn't stop when I wanted to—*except* heroin."

From that point on, the cycle of relapse and recovery raised its ugly head far too frequently. Dealing with heroin was literally like dealing with a demon: a possession or obsession that took over its host. I could often tell that Micah was in relapse long before he would admit it. With my naked eyes, I could see a large, dark blob in his energy field, which I had learned I could chase away with God's power and light. These blobs stayed away as long as I was nearby, but as soon as Micah was away from me, they returned as fast as flies to roadkill.

Whenever Micah was in recovery, he put his all into it. His addictive personality drove his desire to do well, to take care of his physical body, to reconnect to his spiritual nature, and to learn to live daily life without drugs. He never wanted for female companionship, and his charismatic behavior seemed to land him many really nice young women—whether he was in recovery or relapse!

I often spoke to him about learning to live alone, to stand on his own two feet, and to make his way through life without needing someone else in his life. But we finally both admitted it was futile—and like it or not, we deduced that this was a character trait he had received from his father.

Following one of his stints in rehab, Micah met a young professional woman, Michele, in Boone, North Carolina. Michele, an ER nurse, was from Maine, but she had been convinced by one of her childhood friends to make the move to North Carolina to work

Micah and Michele hit it off and quickly became a couple. With the early loss of her father and now her experience as a nurse, Michele was not new to the waves of relapse and recovery in addiction. Like everyone who loved Micah, she was as understanding and available as one could possibly be, and she loved him wholeheartedly.

26

Affirming Life

One morning, just about the time my alarm usually went off, the phone rang—it was Micah. I knew he was in a good place; otherwise, he never would have been up at that time of day. It was early 2005, and he had been doing well from what I could tell.

His voice was excited and somewhat high pitched as he told me about the lucid dream he had just awakened from. He said, "Michele is going to have a baby, and she doesn't even know it now! I saw stairs leading up to a door. Along the walls, kind of like graffiti, I saw the name Skylar. Mom! I am not loaded, and I am not imaging this. It was real! We are going to have a baby, and it's going to be a girl named Skylar!"

I joined in his excitement, and I let him know that I believed him because I knew that often in clear states of mind, we get messages or revelations from our dreams. Intuitively, I felt he saw the possibilities for what his life could be like—and that another soul had agreed to share the journey with him.

His precognition came true. In November 2005, after a very long and arduous labor for Michele, the midwife cleared the baby's mouth and then, looking at Micah, asked if he would like to deliver his child. Without hesitation, he shouted yes!

I was blessed to be in the birthing suite along with the other grandmother-to-be and one of Michele's closest friends. From my vantage point, I could see a conical-shaped, pale purple light precede the physical delivery, and I knew this was a spiritually powerful event.

Frankly, I was surprised to see Micah jump in, seizing the opportunity. I thought he would be squeamish at the sight of blood, but no. He gracefully placed his ungloved hands on the baby, gently pulling the new little human out as if he knew exactly what he was doing. Then abruptly, he roared, "It's a girl!" With the umbilical cord still attached, he gently placed her on Michele's chest, keeping one hand on the baby and putting the other arm around Michele.

Uncontrollable tears of joy flowed from my eyes. The miracle of life and the experience of witnessing the birth of my granddaughter—delivered by her father, whom I'm certain she had met long before she entered this plane—was a Divine blessing.

Skylar had arrived!

27

Across the Generations

At about 5:30 in New York City one early summer afternoon in June 2006, I crawled into the backseat of a black limo sent to take my bank colleagues and me to LaGuardia. I had just settled comfortably into my space when my phone rang. The prefix was 713, which I knew was somewhere in the general Houston vicinity, but I didn't recognize the number. After about four or five rings, I answered.

It was my mother. She had gone to the Methodist Hospital at Texas Medical Center for a cardiac stress test and angioplasty and was supposed to call when she knew something. "Hey, Min," the weak voice on the other end managed to eke out. "I wanted to catch you before you got on your plane to let you know they're keeping me."

"For what?" I asked.

"They're going to do bypass surgery early tomorrow morning."

My heart sank when I heard this, because something told me that my mother was ready to leave this earth. The little voice inside was somehow trying to prepare me. For the past three years, I had used my skills to help my mother heal past hurts and traumas, and in doing so, I had developed an emotional closeness with and compassion for her. I loved her more now than ever before.

"I'll get there as soon as I can," I assured her.

I picked up the phone and called my son, telling him the results of his grandmother's tests and what she would be facing the next day. I could feel his anxiety and fear; he was very close to both his grandmother, Mema, and his grandfather, Dado. Immediately, he said he wanted to go with me to Houston.

At the time, he was clean and sober. He'd been attending college in Boone, and so far, he had straight As in classes like anatomy, physiology, and biochemistry. The semester was close to its end, meaning finals were around the corner, but in no way would he miss being there for Mema and Dado.

Things were going great for him, and he was actually present for me; it was times like this that kept me intact. However, on the flip side, my mother was facing the most serious event in her life.

Once in the hospital maze, we searched for Mema. Exhausted, we finally found Dado and a few cousins sitting in a cardiac surgery waiting room tucked away in a small dark corner.

Micah and I proceeded through the "Authorized Personnel Only—Do Not Enter" doorway, where we were met by a patient coordinator who was making her way to the cardiac waiting room to see if we had arrived yet. They were ready to take my mother into surgery.

Whew! We had barely made it to her bedside!

Thankfully, she was fully coherent, and the authorities allowed us ten minutes with her. The three of us said our prayers, held each other, and gave each other giant, loving, teddy-bear hugs until it was time to take her away.

I looked into the depths of her soul, feeling it would be the last time I would see her in the physical world. Then Micah and I held hands, heads down, as we pensively walked to the waiting room to join our family members, as well as those of others who were having bypass surgery.

Unfortunately, several people in a very short timeframe were told that their loved one had died. Never before had any of us experienced such fear, angst, apprehension, and sorrow—for our fellow waiting-room friends and for ourselves. Every time the door opened, we knew we could be next. The remaining hours were torturous.

Eight long hours later, the door opened. Our bodies shook from the excessive black coffee intake. "Jewel Bailey," the voice beckoned, and we all moved toward the private room. We crammed into the small space, anxiously awaiting the outcome. Time seemed to stand still as we waited for the doctor's mouth to open and tell us what had happened.

"The surgery went well. The blockage was worse than we originally believed, so she had triple bypass surgery and will be in the cardiac critical-care unit for the next several days. Her body is small, but she did just fine."

The relief I felt was like taking off a girdle I had been wearing for days. Part of me felt guilty that my loved one had lived, given the losses of other families in the waiting room; another part reminded me that we were not out of the woods yet. But for the moment, all was well.

★ ★ ★

Three days later, Micah went back to North Carolina to complete his finals and to be with his family. I stayed.

My mother was kept unconscious most of the time so that her body could initiate the healing process. I performed energy-medicine healing on her frail little body—slowly and gently each day. She was 80 years of age, weighed 110 pounds, and was 5 feet 11 inches tall, with upright posture, high cheek bones, beautiful green eyes, and shoulder-length silver hair streaked with occasional jet black left from her Native American roots. She really was a beautiful woman, although I had never viewed her that way before.

Micah called three or more times a day, constantly wanting to know how she was doing—and I believe, more important, how my father, his Dado, was doing. The two of them would talk "man talk"; their bond was strong and definitely beyond my comprehension. It was almost as if Micah represented the son my parents had lost less than twenty-four hours after his birth in 1949.

Born on February 13, the baby named John Parker Bailey Jr. died on February 14.

★ ★ ★

Jewel got stronger and was starting to rebuild her strength when, one Tuesday afternoon around 2:00, she had a stroke that was not diagnosed until the following Friday evening. Over the next weeks and months, she got progressively worse. But she always knew each of us, no matter how bad things got.

Micah returned with Michele and Skylar to be with us as much as possible. On occasion, they would also drive across town to spend time with Michael in the Alzheimer's unit. Michael had always wanted a granddaughter—but now that he had one, could he even realize it? Mysteriously, my mother often asked to see Michael.

My mother seemed really happy despite the impact of the stroke. Her face would glow whenever she held Skylar, and on one of their visits, Micah and Michele told us there would be another great-grandbaby coming in the spring. Naturally, we were elated—and hopeful that Mema would be around to hold the newest member of the family.

Unfortunately, three months after her surgery on September 21, she had a massive cerebral hemorrhage and passed away quietly, in no pain.

★ ★ ★

Over the next days, we planned her funeral service. Micah was overwrought with emotional pain and devastation but was very proud to serve as a pallbearer. He was unable to enter the visitation room while the casket was open; he knew his Mema was not there, and he couldn't bear to pretend that she was the illusion lying in that room.

Somehow, I mustered enough strength to speak at her service. I included the song "In My Daughter's Eyes" by Martina McBride, which said it all:

> *...When I'm gone, I hope you'll see,*
> *How happy she made me,*
> *For I'll be there, in my daughter's eyes.*

I knew the time had come for me to be the reflection of my mother that everyone knew and loved. Through me, she lived on. The umbilical cord had been cut for good. Life would be different. I was now the elder.

When we got in the car to drive to the cemetery, Micah wept and wept. "Mom, I don't see how you could stand up there and do what you just did. It was hard enough to hear the things you said about Mema, but when that song played, all I could think about was Skylar and how much I love her—how true the words of the song are for me and how much I want to live on in her eyes. Mom, I really want to be clean and sober."

Neither of us could stop crying. We exited the car, holding each other as we walked to the graveside—melding soul to soul for what seemed an eternity as little ten-month-old Skylar smiled, gazing with curiosity and fascination as she peered at us over her mother's shoulder.

28

Michael Leaves for the Last Time

In February 2007, I made a trip to Texas to check in on my father and to visit Michael before leaving for a three-week work assignment in Beijing.

I entered the somber atmosphere of Michael's room. His caregiver was sitting in a chair beside the bed. Gleefully, I shouted, "Mr. Felcman! It's Mrs. Felcman! How the hell are you? I am so happy to see you."

Surprisingly, Michael's limp, dying body responded by jerking his torso and kicking his legs. As I approached his bare, diapered body, the caregiver said she had not seen that much life in him since she'd been tending him. I gently placed my hand on his right foot, then along his body up to his shoulder. I leaned over and kissed him on his forehead.

The cloudy fog in his eyes cleared, and they glistened brilliantly, as if to acknowledge that he recognized me. I talked to him, letting him know how much I loved him. His eyes faded from cloudy to cataract-like and then back to clear.

In those moments of clarity, I felt his soul. I stayed with him, continuously leaving one hand on his body for three-and-a-half hours. I helped the caregiver change his diaper—something I would never have conceived of doing for a spouse. The cycle of life was so present in my being; before my eyes, Michael was close to the end of this lifetime.

Every hurt, pain, and disappointment I had experienced with him seemed to dissolve and blow away like sand on the desert. Somehow, the only thing I could feel was forgiveness and unconditional love— one human to another.

Michael passed away March 29, 2007, one day before my return from China.

29

The Circle of Life

Much like a revolving door, the death of one family member was met with the birth of another. On April 17, 2007, Parker Felcman was born to Michele and Micah. Dado was especially proud and happy to have a great-grandson carry his middle name, Parker.

I had planned to be present for the birth, but with my return from China, the work that accompanied it, travel to Texas for Michael's funeral, and the undue demands of a job that seemed to work me twenty-four hours a day, I was working against the clock for a deliverable required of me before leaving Charlotte. Coupled with a much shorter labor for Michele than expected, I was late getting to the hospital and totally missed my new grandchild's entrance.

He was cleaned up, wrapped, and ready for this Grannie's arms once I entered the room. Strangely, something about the "air" between Micah and Michele felt off. I blew it off to the stress and exhaustion of delivery.

★ ★ ★

One evening around ten o'clock, just before the Easter holiday, I received a disturbing phone call from Michele telling me that Micah was in the intensive care unit of the hospital in Boone—and the doctors didn't know if he would make it through the night. She was calling to ask if I could please get there as soon as possible—she had the two children and could not be at the hospital with Micah.

I grabbed a set of clothes and the dog and sped off on the two-and-a-half-hour drive to Boone. Just before entering town, I was stopped by a police officer. In tears, I pleaded for him to let me go. I needed to get to my son in Watagua County Hospital and asked if he would lead me there. He agreed, and my last few minutes' drive was much faster than I had traveled thus far. By now, it was midnight.

I parked the car, leaving the dog, Jazz, to fend for herself. Making my way to the intensive care unit, I found Micah. As I opened the door, he looked at me and said, "Mom, I have really messed up this time. I am really sick, and I don't think I'm going to be able to make it."

By now, I had been through so many of these near-death experiences that my being was completely in neutral. I pulled up a seat beside the bed; looked closely at the monitors; read the labels on the IV lines; watched the P, QRS, and T waves on the electrocardiogram; and wondered how it was that he was so severely ill.

About that time, a doctor entered the room, telling me as she approached that he had sepsis and that the likelihood of his survival through the night was nil. It would be OK for me to sit by his bedside for the remainder of the night, and the staff would be just outside the door. She then left.

I looked at Micah and asked him if he was ready to die. Tears rolled from those big brown eyes as he shook his head in the negative and weakly cried, "No! no! no!" I asked him to hold my hand, and we prayed. He drifted off. I never let go of his hand. I could tell he went very deep around 3:00 a.m.

Suddenly, his body jerked, his motions were odd, and the sounds coming from his mouth were like none I had ever heard. I felt he was leaving, crossing over, and I wanted to hold a sacred space to make his transition as smooth as possible. How was I able to do this? I have no clue. It's what I felt guided to do.

After two hours in this space, Micah came to. He looked surprised, as if he expected to be somewhere else. His eyes looked

110

me up and down as if to register my reality. He looked at our hands, still interlocked. He looked around the room as if he had just realized he was still here. He turned his head toward me, crying, telling me he wanted to live. He wanted to be there for his kids, he wanted to quit drugs, he wanted to travel and visit family loved ones—and he wanted me to be a part of their lives.

He started crying out loudly for Skylar. "I want to see my daughter! I want to see my daughter! Please bring her to me. I love her and I need to see her!"

He got so loud that the staff came into the room to see what was going on. They assured him she could visit him later in the morning.

"How?" he commanded.

They said, "She can come to the waiting room, and we will wheel you out there in a wheelchair. We promise you, you can see and hold your children later this morning."

Assured he would have the chance to hold both Skylar and Parker, he drifted off to sleep, squeezing my hand more tightly, as if to say, "Don't let me go."

Two days later, he was moved from critical care to a regular room. He stayed there for one week while being given intravenous antibiotics. A week later, he was able to go home and continue the IV antibiotics there. Fortunately, this was possible because Michele was a nurse and knew what to do.

Once Micah recovered, he and Michele loaded up the kids, and off they went, living life's adventures. First, they drove to Orlando, Florida, to visit Christopher, who now preferred to be called by his first name, John. From there they made their way across the United States to Texas, where they set up base camp at Dado's house. They traversed Texas, traveling south to visit all of Michael's living relatives—meeting cousins, aunts, and uncles, and reconnecting to Micah's roots.

Once their travels to the South were completed, they boarded an airplane for Maine, where they made similar rounds.

I never knew what caused the sepsis.

30

Heartbreak

Life seemed to be going great when suddenly, things hit a brick wall. In early Spring 2008, Micah and Michele split, and she left for Maine with the children. Micah was in school at the time and wanted to finish the semester before moving to Maine to be closer to the children.

I felt something serious had happened between Michele and Micah, but I knew to mind my own business. Knowing Micah the way I did, I was sure that being removed from his children was an emotional blow he likely couldn't handle. He needed something positive to stay focused on, and for now, school was it.

The day Michele, Skylar, and Parker drove out of town, he called me, sobbing hysterically. I could feel the deep emotional pain in every cell of his body. I was in Charlotte, and he was in Boone. I wanted to hold him, but there was nothing I could do but let him talk and cry. I sensed he would not be able to hold himself together for very long and that relapse would be imminent; if it hadn't already happened, it would just be a matter of time.

In June 2008, I remarried. I had lived alone for fifteen years, and somehow, I finally felt I could marry again. I felt a deep soul connection with my new mate and partner, Rock, and I was ready to enter into sacred union.

Unfortunately, Micah could not hold it together to be sober during my wedding festivities. His behavior was indicative of an addict in relapse: he was anxious and nervous, he was unable to engage with others, and he spent much of the time pacing or in absentia. He abandoned his date during the rehearsal dinner, where his behavior was beyond appalling.

I was deeply hurt and upset that he could not be present for this important life event of mine, and I believed that because of his behavior, I did not have the blessing of having my grandchildren at my wedding. But though my heart wanted my son to share this special day with me, I had always maintained airtight boundaries around his addiction. When he called me the next morning, my wedding day, I told him I didn't want him around me.

My heart was broken, and my body writhed and ached. This was supposed to be the happiest day of my life. Family and friends from around the world had traveled to Charlotte to share my wedding day, and here I was a complete wreck.

Lee, my matron of honor, was with me. In a gentle voice, she said, "Mindy, what is really in your heart?"

"I want my son to be with me today. I love him, and I want him to share this day with me," I wailed.

"Then call him and tell him you love him and want him to be with you," Lee suggested firmly.

So I phoned him back and left a message telling him how much I loved him. I knew he had relapsed, but I welcomed him at my wedding. I asked that he hold it together to be there for me.

I had no idea whether he would be there or not until I came upstairs from the bride's room and saw him standing at the top of the stairs with my father, both waiting to walk me down the aisle.

In July, Micah married a young woman named Amber. I believe he married her at this time because he knew he could not have his children stay with him if he had a live-in girlfriend. Also, Micah, like Michael, was not good at being alone, so this marriage gave

Micah someone to be in Maine with him. But who am I to say how he experienced love? He was accepted into the Surgery Technology program at Maine Medical in Portland, but unfortunately, he had to wait several months to begin—not a good thing for someone battling addiction.

Having too much time on his hands led him to the most serious relapse I had witnessed to date. It was in the spring of 2009 that he left his wife, loaded up his SUV, drove to Charlotte, and sold his vehicle for drugs and an airplane ticket to Hawaii—where I felt he was certain to die.

31

Hope

Out of the blue on July 4, 2009, I received a call from Micah asking if I could pick him up from a rehabilitation facility in Wilkesboro, North Carolina. Shocked and astounded that he had made it back from Hawaii alive—and that he had taken the steps to clean up after this lengthy relapse—I agreed to pick him up to take him to a halfway house. I had done the drill so many times; I knew this was his way of asking for forgiveness and reconnecting with me to start over again.

I drove him to a halfway house not far away in Newton, North Carolina; he had nothing but the borrowed clothes on his back. My heart hurt every time I turned to leave. Why did life have to be this way? Why couldn't he beat this disease? He seemed to be a trooper at starting over—much stronger than me in so many ways.

Unfortunately, his struggle with heroin was severe, and his ability to get a grip was lessening. Anytime I was around him, I could see the dark beings in his field. It seems they had a vice grip on him, and nothing was working to stop them. I could tell Micah's ability to mentally fight these beings was also diminishing, and it was hard for me to see him unable to do anything more about it.

Within four months, he was back in rehab, this time for a longer time. The next call I received was to spend New Year's Eve with him in Wilmington, North Carolina, at his latest halfway house. He wanted to start the New Year off right and asked Rock and me to be with him. Rock, Harmony (our dog), and I delightfully made the four-hour drive to spend the holiday with him.

One thing I learned on this journey of addiction is to never give up hope. As long as there is life, there is hope, and all it takes is a small sliver of light to turn things around. I was happy to support my son in every way possible whenever that sliver appeared.

32

Death's-Door Choice

In April 2010, Micah had had as much of Wilmington as his restless being could handle, so he packed up and struck out for San Diego, California, to spend time with his good friend Will and hopefully land a decent job. The heroin and his struggle to avoid it were really working him hard. I had to let him go—literally—or I would be the one to die.

My experiences became so "gut-wrenching" that I ended up having an emergency appendectomy in May; ten days later, I returned to the hospital with a small bowel obstruction that nearly took my life. In the early hours of the morning the day after my second surgery, I had what I call a death's-door choice. It was not a near-death experience or anything that resembles the stories of near-death experiences. I found myself led by two tall white human-like beings to the edge of vast blackness—like a giant blank TV screen that went on infinitely both vertically and horizontally. Instantaneously, I recognized one of the beings as Pat, a guy I went to grade school with who had passed away decades ago.

"What is going on?" I asked. With no verbal answer, he continued nodding for me to move toward the blackness and step in. "Why?" I queried. "Because it's time," he responded, both verbally and telepathically. "Will it hurt?" I asked, with great concern. "No, it won't hurt; I promise," he assured me. I felt as if he was coaching me but could not tell me what to do. I had to be the one to step into the vast abyss. After great hesitation, I stepped toward the blackness. With each step, I could feel everything associated with being "Mindy" fading. Startled, I stopped, abruptly realizing I was losing the "me" I'd known for years—my ego was rapidly dissolving!

Pat observed my hesitation and gently said, "Go on, and keep moving. I promise it will not hurt." Just like taking one arm at a time out of a pullover sweater, I proceeded into the black vastness, losing more and more of myself. By the time I had passed fully into this blackness, I could tell that I was one with all that is.

I was alone but sensed other presences around me—and a oneness. I felt nothing but pure bliss—I was part of the vastness. Much like a cup of water poured into the ocean, the "Mindy shell" was gone, and the essence of my being was reunited with all. There was no emotion, only silence as I realized my immateriality, my formlessness.

Pat stayed on the other side, but somehow I knew if I needed him all I had to do was think it and he would be there. I drifted and floated in my no-gravity space. After playing and experiencing myself in this manner, I heard Pat ask if I wanted to come back. "I don't know yet," I responded through thought. "OK, if you decide you want to come back, just come back through to the left of where you entered," he instructed.

After toying around in timelessness, I decided to go back. Re-entering through the "left side," I could feel myself forming into material substance the closer I got to my point of entry. Stepping through, I became liquid light, molding back into the old ego Mindy—same clothes and all. Like a cup of water being scooped from the ocean. I felt exhilarated and quickly told Pat, who was right there to greet me, that it had not hurt. I felt so ecstatic I decided to do it again and again. I have clear recall of going through the same process three more times, each time staying longer and longer in the bliss and oneness.

It was a choice. I had reached a point in life where I could either stay here or go on. As I toyed with the idea of going on, I experienced what that felt like. In doing so, I realized I had not done what I felt called to do in this life; there was something left for me to do. Exactly what it was, I didn't know, but whatever it was, it was just for me—not for my son, not for my aging father, not for my spouse, and not for my grandchildren.

When I awoke, returning from a place of bliss and oneness—presumably the same place Micah visited when he had sepsis—my mother's spirit descended upon me, gently caressing my face and kissing my forehead before drifting away. I realized she was there to escort me should I have chosen to cross over.

On May 18, Micah phoned Rock. He knew something was seriously wrong if his mother didn't call him on his birthday. I had tubes down my throat and couldn't speak, so Rock filled him in on the severity of my condition. I got out of the hospital on Memorial Day and began my road to recovery, starting with learning how to eat all over again.

In June, Micah made his way from San Diego to Dado's house in Texas. On June 21, Dado would be ninety years old, and the whole family was going to gather to celebrate. Fortunately, my staples came out and the doctor gave me the go-ahead to make the trip.

I saw Micah in Texas—he looked good. He seemed to be settling into a routine with Dado. But as Micah's luck would have it, it was not long before he was on the run again. He made it back to North Carolina, but not without having an accident that caused his car to be impounded and left him in Georgia. There was a huge error with his insurance coverage, and unfortunately, he was grossly mistreated given the offense. It seemed he had a large, black cloud over him.

Once back in Boone, he settled into his drug den and slid further and further down the hole. Getting himself back into rehab was the best thing he did, and from there, he made his way back to Wilmington. He had not seen Skylar and Parker since his relapse and departure from Maine in 2009, and Michele was less than amenable when it came to allowing him to talk to them. So in September 2010, the children came to visit Rock and me in Charlotte.

Micah came in from Wilmington, and over the next several days, the five of us had the best time anyone could imagine. His love for his children exuded from his body. They played and shared a depth of being like I had never seen before. When it was time for them to leave, Micah could not stop crying. He hugged and squeezed them tightly, as if he knew he would never see them again. I encouraged him to be a bit more lighthearted and focus on the next time they could get together. I suggested he might want to go to Maine for Skylar's birthday in November.

On December 30, 2010, Micah and a young woman companion visited Rock and me in Charlotte, before we headed uptown to take black-and-white photos of him reading poetry at the intersection of Trade and Tryon. Little did I know that would be the last time I would ever see him in physical form.

33

March 29, 2011

In March of 2011, I planned a trip to Texas to work with one of my teacher-healers. I spoke with my father to let him know when I would be there, and much to my surprise, he informed me that Micah would be there also. He didn't know the specifics of Micah's journey to Texas, but he believed Micah wanted to start life over again.

Micah called me when he found out I would be there too. He had been in bad relapse since early January, so my contact with him had been nil. I told him I'd be around, but I was doubtful that I would be at my father's house at the same time as Micah would be.

★ ★ ★

The phone rang, waking me from a sleep that I had had a hard time falling into in the first place. I was in the Woodlands, Texas, at my dear friend and healer's house, with the intention of beginning an intensive three-day study the next day. I rolled over to answer the phone, and it was Will Black, Micah's friend who lived in San Diego. *Why is he ringing me in the wee hours of the night?* I thought.

"I've been on the phone with Micah much of the night. He is at Dado's house on the porch with a loaded gun and a bottle of whiskey. I have been talking to him for hours, but nothing seems to help. He doesn't believe you love him. I kept telling him how much I know you love him, but somehow, it didn't seem to register. I can tell he has been drinking, and this time, he sounds very different. I just didn't know what to do, so I called you. I'm sorry to bother you, but I thought this was pretty important. I thought about calling 911, but I'm in San Diego, and he's in Liberty—I don't even know where, other than 'Dado's house.'"

As my mind tried to wrap itself around what I was hearing, my body raised itself to attention in the bed. How many times had I dealt with the crises of addiction? I asked Will to tell me what he and Micah had talked about to see if I could get a grip on my son's state.

Will gave me a synopsis of their hours of dialogue. Good friend that Will was, he had wanted to keep talking to Micah, to keep him uplifted, and to do his best to connect to him. "But when Micah got into you, his mother, not loving him, nothing I could say could make him change the way he was talking," he said. Will asked me if it was OK for him to phone Micah back and tell him that I definitely loved him and wanted to talk with him.

Will and I had both been through addiction crises with Micah before, and I understood that Will was asking me what to do now because this time was different. He was checking in with me, wanting to validate his actions—and inactions. Things had been tough at other times, but this time, it was time to get Mother Mindy involved.

"Yes, of course, by all means call him back," I said with deep concern.

I lay there, staring at the ceiling and the brilliant colors in the room. I wanted to fade into the colors, to disappear into the vibration of the bright purple and golden yellow. I did my best to maintain my composure, as I had done for more than fifteen years while trying to understand and handle my son's drug addiction. But something inside me also said that this time was different.

I was pulled from my thoughts by the phone ringing again. This time it was Micah.

"You'll take a call from Will in the middle of the night, but you won't take one from me," he said flatly.

I responded, "I'm talking to you now. I want you to know that I love you more than you will ever know."

"I don't believe you," he replied, again with very flat intonation.

Hurriedly, I searched my heart for the words that I needed to say and that I felt he desperately needed to hear.

"I do love you. You are very precious to me. I believe it would be a good idea for you to get back to North Carolina so you can get the help you need."

In the short time it took for me to get those words out, I realized he had hung up.

This time I stared at the purple and golden yellow ceiling in a different way. *Dear God, I pleaded, please hold my son, Micah Aaron Matthew Felcman, in your arms through this night. Let the highest good for him be done.* How many times over fifteen years had I pleaded the same prayer to God...?

Falling asleep again seemed impossible. My mind ran aimlessly in so many directions. I pondered dialing 911 and providing the address in Liberty, but something inside me said, *If you do, he will be picked up, put into a psychiatric facility, and probably turned loose in less than twenty-four hours—and the cycle will start all over AGAIN!*

I thought about running out of the house and driving the one-and-a-half hours to my father's house, but a voice said, "Don't! You don't want to find him or see him *if* he has 'done something.' You don't want to revive him only to have him end up a vegetable. He would never want that." So, again, I gave my son to his Creator—to God—and asked that I be held also, no matter what happened. I surrendered my being, my essence to the Divine.

All I could do was love him, love him, love him. I sensed he felt he had done wrong, was off track, and had lost respect and worthiness in my eyes. I had to let go of my fear in order to love unconditionally.

I lost track of the minutes and the seconds—and eventually, I drifted back to sleep.

I was abruptly awakened by a loud ring again—and again, it was not my alarm! I fumbled to find my phone, slowly realizing I was not in my familiar surroundings. It appeared to be 6:40 a.m.

Still somewhat discombobulated, I could nevertheless make out that the number on the phone was that of my father. With a very tired and worn-out voice, I answered, "Hello."

On the other end, I heard, "Mindy, Matt's dead."

"No, he's not!" I snapped.

"Yes, he is," my father said in a monotone voice.

John, my father, is the most easygoing, most even-keeled person I have ever known in my life. The earth could separate thirty feet in front of him, and his demeanor, personality, and approach would never waiver. But he's not too good with the emotional stuff: he's from the generation that was taught that men don't cry.

This time I yelled, "No, he is not!" The monotone voice on the other end of the phone stated again, "Yes, he is. Matt's dead."

Again I screamed, "NO, HE IS NOT!"

The monotone voice of my father—John, Dado, grandfather of Micah—went up an octave with his next words, "WELL, HE DAMN SURE IS! I am sitting here looking at him with blood coming out of his mouth! He is cold and purple. The police are on their way now; how long until you can get here?"

In shock, I said, "I don't know. I'll be there as soon as I can."

"Ok, drive safely. I'll see you shortly," he said, again in that monotone voice.

When I hung up the phone, my entire being felt something that no words in any language on this planet could describe. I felt like a cornucopia, a kaleidoscope of feelings, emotions, and thoughts, with visions of threadlike colors racing through the cells of my body in directions I never knew existed, all at once. I was paralyzed, I was relieved—I even felt freedom for my son, as odd as that may seem. My mind raced through our lives together. I stared at the purple and golden yellow colors on the ceiling and asked God to take me through the next steps.

The most profound feeling I experienced was my heart bursting into millions of shattered pieces! I cried and cried from the depths of my heart and my very existence on this earth. The fabric of my essence ached. The wailing of this mother echoed across the globe. For more than fifteen years, I had fought addiction and my son had fought addiction—and at that second, I felt a giant sucker punch hit me in my stomach.

Had we really lost the fight? Had he lost, or had he fulfilled his soul's purpose with me? Was it time for him to move on to higher, greater soul duties? What did all of this mean—other than that I would never see my son in the physical form I had known for almost thirty-two years? Rationalization . . . I needed something to grab on to.

Damn it! I had done everything I knew how to help him—not to enable him, but to walk in love beside him and not interfere in his path—yet somehow, I felt I had completely lost. All the years of pain I had borne with steadfast courage had been for naught. I had walked through every challenge, believing I was growing and learning each time. Had I just been kidding myself?

I am not a fierce competitor in this material world, but in the spiritual world, nothing is out of bounds for me. During this journey with my son, as I described earlier, I had faced many negative energy forms in as fierce a fight as any superhero had ever jumped into. The difference was that my fight was for what I believe matters in the spiritual world while living an earthly life.

What was really happening? My son, my miracle was . . . gone?

My heart had more than exploded, but something inside me felt I had to "hold things together." After all, I had studied spiritual teachings for years, and practice is what grounds and solidifies these teachings as we walk on earth. Right? Right. Wasn't I literally experiencing what Jesus walked this planet to teach us?

But for some reason, I had grave difficulties understanding. Never before had Mother Mary's pain at seeing her son on the cross hit me as it did in this moment. The heart that once sat on a shelf because the pain was so great had been gradually and gently reintegrated into my body, and now, in less than a second, it had been shattered into a million pieces, each with its own hologram of pain.

Somehow, I held myself together enough to find Petrene, my teacher and healer, and convey to her what had happened. The second I walked into her house (next door to the clients' house where I was staying), she could see the energetic malfunction in my energy field and asked me to sit down at the kitchen table while she made me a cup of coffee. I was in shock and didn't even realize it!

My mind wandered to my son, reflecting on times past. Each time it did, she would bring me back to the present, making certain I did not slip into severe emotional trauma. For the next two hours, she kept me right in front of her, watching closely to make sure I was absorbing the information of my son's death in the best light possible.

As I tried to get up to leave and get to my father's house in Liberty, she asked me to sit tight. She had phoned my close childhood friend, Lee, to let her know what had happened and to ask her to come and be with me, if at all possible. Lee showed up with our other childhood friend, Marie, and together, the four of us sat at Petrene's kitchen table, digesting what had happened.

While no one spoke it, I knew in my heart the three of them were keeping me at that kitchen table long enough for the police and medics to get to my father's house and handle the situation. The last thing I needed or wanted was to see my child being placed in a body bag and carried off by total strangers. God bless my father: he had found Micah and witnessed everything from that point on.

Every so often, Petrene would look at me as though she were looking through me and would then strongly suggest I eat the special porridge she had made for me. Bite by bite, I consumed the concoction, which grounded me and calmed the butterflies in my stomach.

When Petrene gave the thumbs-up that it was OK for me to leave, Marie slipped behind the wheel of my rental car, and Lee followed closely behind. The drive was surreal . . . my son was dead, and I was being chauffeured to the scene. No one else knew—no other family members or friends, nor any of Micah's.

The drive from the Woodlands to Liberty was long, but not nearly as long as crossing the Trinity River Bridge—the first hint of reality that I was entering the town of Liberty and was headed to my father's house. We were passing landmarks indicating we were getting closer and closer to the home I grew up in, now the home with the doorway where my son had taken his life. The closer we got, the faster my heart raced and the tighter my body felt. *Breathe,* I said to myself, *deeply and slowly,* as Marie made the turn onto Newman Street.

Slowly, we approached my father's house. Cars were all over the street, with several pulled up into the yard. Micah's female companion and her five dogs were meandering around the yard in a total fog. People were standing around the yard—some crying softly and some just in shock. I noticed that the front door was open and that two women were madly shampooing the bloodstained carpet at the front-door entrance.

As I approached, the onlookers parted, making a path so I could pass. I reached the sacred place where my son had crossed over. My immediate response was to lay my body over the two front doorsteps and the entryway into the house, where what was left of my son's life force remained in the carpet.

As I lay there, tears gently falling down my cheeks, I used all of the energy I could muster to ask God to show me what had happened. As I did, I saw my son's spirit—his soul—exit his body at a very rapid speed through the top of his head, micromillimeters ahead of the image of the bullet. I saw a white energy form—much like that of the forceful, dense steam from boiling water—freed from the confines and bounds of the human body. I felt him soar. More and more tears flowed as I realized he was experiencing the freedom he had desperately needed and longed for.

I asked God if any part of Micah was "hung" in that place in my father's house or in this dimension, to which I heard a resounding

"No!" I picked myself up off the floor and made my way over to my father's chair to hold him, hug him, and love him. He looked at me and shook his head in his quirky, angular manner, accompanied by a shoulder shrug. I had seen that gesture several times before, but this time, it was larger than ever. To me it was indicative of his being unable to do anything with emotions.

Nonetheless, I hugged him tightly, as he said, "Now Mindy, stop crying."

34

Accepting Death

Now what? My son was gone, and I had no idea where his body was. I phoned the numbers on a piece of paper my father had, only to find out that Micah's body had been taken to a nearby town for an autopsy. I was instructed to sit tight and was told that I would be contacted within three days.

I found out the names of the detectives who were at the scene; I phoned them and asked if I could meet with them. They agreed, and I found their words to be quite comforting. They told me what they had found at the scene and explained the process I would need to go through, informing me that the autopsy results could take up to ninety days. In the meantime, my son's belongings would be with them until the case was closed. There were no suicide notes or evidence of a planned decision, despite being the same day Michael died four years earlier.

I could not have made it through those slow, emotionally painful, and grueling days without the love, comfort, and presence of my cousin Kay. She arrived late on the afternoon of March 29 and did not leave my side, day or night.

Early in the afternoon of the third day after Micah's death, the phone rang at my father's house. I answered and heard a male voice announcing himself to be from Broussard's Mortuary. For some reason, the gentleman told me the bullet never exited the head, the autopsy was complete, and the body was ready for identification.

As soon as I heard those words, my legs weakened severely. I told the voice on the other end of the phone that I could not possibly see my son. The pain was far too great, and the sight of his body was a vision I simply did not want imprinted in my mind. I asked him if he would describe my son—specifically his tattoos—and whether that would suffice as proper identification of the body. Thankfully, he said yes and proceeded to describe Micah's body.

"There is a sleeve on his left arm with a large koi swimming upstream, indicative of struggle. The tattoo is in red, yellow, and green. He has a spiderweb in black on his elbow." My legs failed me as I heard this strange voice using almost the same words and language my son had used to tell me why he had gotten each tattoo and what each one meant. The voice continued, "On his chest, there are two doves, one with 'Skylar 11-9-2005' on one side and 'Parker 4-17-2007' on the other side."

"Without a doubt, that's my son," I mustered in a faint voice. I had just identified my son's body over the phone—it was as though he had been dictating his own life's description vis-à-vis his tattoos.

I could take no more of this reality, and I collapsed on the hallway floor into the guttural sobs, deep pain, and emotional trauma Petrene had tried to help me avoid earlier. What I did not know was that this was just the beginning of the waves of emotion I would feel over the next hours, days, weeks, months—and ultimately, years.

The waiting continued. It would be at least another two to three days before the ashes would be ready. I was promised another call when they were en route.

The day came. Kay and I sat on the couch looking out of the double-paned windows at the front of the house. My heart leapt into my throat as a large black limousine pulled up outside. Kay gently squeezed my hand as I got up, walked to the front door, and crossed the threshold where my son had died. I moved toward the stranger who held the remains of my child.

I couldn't feel my feet on the ground at all; it was almost as though I were floating out to meet the gentleman from Broussard's. Our eyes met at the same time I noticed the box he carried. He began extending it toward me. In what seemed like slow motion, I reached out my arms to take my son's ashes.

As I did, I fell into a momentary time warp. I was awash with a magnificent presence and knowing. In a matter of milliseconds, I traversed the world, observing and sensing mothers receiving the remains of their children. I saw images of a coffin covered with an American flag, slowly moving down a conveyor belt of an airplane; of an African tribeswoman being handed the body of her son by an elder warrior, who anchored his spear firmly in the ground to honorably make the transfer; of an Asian woman with dark black hair, slanted eyes, and light skin, standing in a field of lush green and stoically receiving information of her daughter's fatal accident; and of the faces of numerous women of other nationalities accepting death, deep sadness, trauma, and immense pain related to the loss of their children. They all passed before me like a movie on fast forward.

I felt our humanness, our alikeness, and our despair as the weight of the box, now firmly in my hands, pulled me out of my altered state. I thanked the gentleman from Broussard's, and I turned and walked away. I was ready to go home.

PART TWO

The Healing:
The Hero Returns

35

The Bead

(April 2011)

Once I received Micah's ashes, I could hardly wait to get back to Charlotte, the place I had by then called home for the past eighteen years. My dear husband, Rock, insisted on sending a jet to Houston to pick up my father and me—and Micah's remains—so that we might privately and honorably make the difficult journey back.

Rock arrived with Harmony, who could not stop licking me and jumping on me. Somehow, she sensed something was hurting me emotionally. I boarded the jet with my son in a box in my arms. Making my way to the back row, I cuddled him as tightly as if he were that newborn papoose I had held thirty-one years prior. Harmony promptly took her place beside me, while Rock and my father took their seats.

The pain coursing through my being was immense, but somehow, I rationalized it away, believing I understood what was happening spiritually. I put my big-girl panties on and proudly flew with the remains of my only child, as though I were a high-ranking air force officer on special assignment.

We arrived at our home in Challis Farm, where we were greeted by several dear friends sitting on the porch steps awaiting our arrival—and by the magnificent beauty of the blankets of while tulips overflowing from the flowerbeds and planters. How all the white tulips ended up in the yard was a mystery. The landscaper knows I love color, and of all the years we have lived in our home, this was the only spring when over one thousand white tulips bloomed.

One by one, still in disbelief, Micah's friends began to arrive, also. When they saw his remains in a box, still tightly guarded by me, the reality became much more than any of them could bear. Seeing them all cry uncontrollably and witnessing the biggest badass of them fall to the floor sobbing ignited my emotions all over again. It took two or three days for me to collect myself enough to be of assistance to the friends who so lovingly planned and prepared Micah's memorial service.

As much as Micah loved nature and the outdoor activities of hunting, fishing, and enjoying the ocean and mountains, he was equally called by the concrete of the city—with its crowds, raging sirens, and round-the-clock pulse. So St. Mary's Chapel in downtown Charlotte was the perfect venue for his service on April 10, 2011. It was standing room only. Several attendees did not even know Micah; they had read his obituary in the local newspaper and showed up at his service to learn more about him!

I was somewhat dumbfounded when I was approached by these strangers asking my permission to sit among Micah's family and friends. But at the same time, I felt honored because this incident was indicative of the charismatic, mysterious charm of Micah's personality and the numerous lives he had touched around the world.

The adults decided that the memorial service would be too much for Micah's young children to attend, so we arranged for the kids to visit a week later, when my full attention and focus could be on them and I could gently introduce them to the death of their Pappa. They had not seen their great-grandfather, Dado, in a long time, and I was hopeful the hurt and pain of Micah's passing could be somewhat alleviated by all of us spending time together.

We attended church on Easter, beginning with a butterfly release and followed by the children singing "Jesus Loves Me." Skylar was particularly observant of the crosses that were everywhere in the church and on the grounds. She knew her Pappa always wore one, and I could see those little wheels turning as she was making the connection. The symbolism of Easter and what "death" meant for Micah was weighing on me heavily.

One afternoon later in the week, two of Micah's best friends, Sinclaire and Tony, brought their children over to play with Skylar and Parker. Surreally, I watched the cycle of life unfolding in front of me, realizing it wasn't that long ago that I had sat on the porch watching Micah, Tony, and Sinclaire as kids on skateboards. The children were having a wonderful time—giggling, running, chasing the dog, and playing ball.

I turned around to walk into the house to go to the bathroom. When I opened the front door, I noticed an eerie silence and peculiar "air" around me. I continued walking toward the bathroom, when suddenly an object dropped right in front of me from somewhere high above my head! It hit the tile floor, bounced high, and rhythmically made its way toward the dining table, where Micah's ashes and altar were.

Immediately, I *knew* Micah was doing his best to get my attention. I chased the bouncing object for what felt like an eternity. Exasperated, I finally managed to grab it—just before it rolled under the dining room hutch. I halted in my footsteps, looking down at a 9 mm bead in my hand.

No one was in the house. Where would a 9 mm bead come from? Why did it drop right in front of me? Why did it roll toward, rather than away from, the altar and Micah's ashes? Why did I know and sense it was him trying desperately to get my attention—and what was it for?

The only thing I could do was acknowledge what had just happened. As I did, I taped the bead to the top of the urn holding Micah's ashes, where it still rests today.

36

Sinclaire's Call

(April 2011)

Approximately three days after the bead incident, on a Wednesday evening, I received a frantic phone call from Sinclaire. She was sobbing so hard I could barely understand her. I had no idea what had happened, but I did all I could do to help calm her down.

Through her tears, she kept saying, "Micah" and "I need to talk to you. I don't understand. I need help." I could hear road noise in the background, and I insisted she pull over immediately. I thought she might have been in an accident and was in shock—but why would she call me and not her mother? Once she pulled over and got still, she began to tell me what had happened.

It was early evening, and she was on her way back to Charlotte from Savannah, Georgia. She was about two-and-a-half hours into the drive when her cell phone, which was in her purse on the floorboard of the passenger side of her SUV, rang. Fumbling to get to the phone while keeping her eye on the road, she finally found it close to the bottom of her bag. When she looked to see who was calling, the LED on her iPhone read *Micah, 808.397.1868.* In horror and disbelief, fighting back tears, she proceeded to answer the phone.

"Hello! Micah, is that you?" she anxiously cried out. "Mmmmiiiiiicccccaaaaahhhhh, SPEAK to me!" she screamed. She waited frantically, but there was nothing—no sound came from the other end, and the call dropped.

As I listened to her, I could not help feeling Micah reaching out to her as he had done with me and the bead. Sinclaire and Micah had been the best of friends since our arrival in Charlotte, and I would not have put it past him to do all he could to communicate with her.

Sinclaire asked if it would be OK for her to come directly to my house. She wanted to show me the phone, and she wanted to talk. I stayed on the phone with her until she felt more settled; we finally hung up when she was about an hour out of Charlotte.

I met her in the driveway, where without getting out of the SUV, she rolled down the window on the driver's side, pushed the phone into my face, and shouted, "Look! Look at this!"

I looked, and sure enough, the phone history showed an incoming call from *Micah, 808.397.1868, at 7:37 p.m.!* I felt chills all over my body as tears began to flow uncontrollably. Sinclaire got out of the SUV, and together, we stood in the driveway, holding each other in trepidation at the mystery we'd experienced that night.

Later, I wondered if someone at the police station could have used his phone to make the call. But the detective I spoke to assured me that Micah's phone was locked up with the gun and his other belongings taken from the scene.

37

The Swing

(May 2011)

Life was going as well as could be expected for a mother who had lost her only child. It was the third week of May. The grandchildren had gone back to Maine, and my father was back in Texas.

Emotionally, I had been through the ringer. I had made it through Easter singing "Jesus Loves Me" with Skylar and Parker in the children's group. I had seen my son's death through the eyes of his young children as they slowly paced in front of his altar, looked at pictures, picked up items of his clothing, put on and took off his sunglasses, tried on his rosaries—and grasped for what had really happened to their Pappa. I had made it through realizing the frailty of my father yet seeing the sheer joy he had when spending time with his great-grandchildren. Through them he was able to see Micah live on.

One thing I noticed about my father was his daily wearing of the rosary that had been passed out at Micah's memorial service. He tied it around the button on his shirt so it hung proudly on his chest. Peculiar, I thought, for I had never seen my father openly embrace religious artifacts, even though I knew he had his own beliefs about God. It seemed to me he was crying out for answers to Micah's death, asking for the release of the horrible images imprinted on his mind and the feelings in his heart after finding Micah in the early morning of March 29. Feelings were something my father was exceptional at stuffing away—but try as he might, these feelings were beyond repressing.

Once everyone had left, I felt I could process and really feel what I'd had to contain earlier. It was dusk, and my girlfriend Anna stopped by for a visit. She and I were sitting on the couch, catching up on the past days' events, when I got up to get us bottles of water out of the pantry.

As I closed the pantry door, through the kitchen window I noticed the swing on the porch moving in a gentle back-and-forth swinging motion. The hair on my neck rose as I watched. Instantly, my brain went into action to determine if there was a wind blowing or if something else was happening that would cause this. My father had made the swing and had just hung it in April, right before Micah's memorial service. I had thought it a good idea for my father to be available to supervise the hanging of his masterpiece and make sure it was done right.

The more I watched the swing, the more it seemed to move. Standing there, glued to the windowpane with two bottles of water in my hands, I shouted, "Anna, come here! Look at the swing!"

"What's the matter?" she asked, as she moved quickly across the room from the couch to the window.

"Look!" I exclaimed histrionically. "Oh, my God," she said in her British accent, "I cannot believe my eyes!"

The two of us stood there, dazed and confused at the movement of the swing. The pace had picked up from when I'd first seen it, so my brain completely dropped the idea that it was being moved by the wind.

The swing was firmly hung on a covered porch and was set pretty far back from the edge near the steps. Nevertheless, my mind continued to swirl in deep conflict— because my heart knew it was Micah trying to contact me or get a message to me.

About the time I deduced this, the swing changed motion and began moving in an elliptical pattern, as though someone were anchoring the heel of one foot and purposefully moving it in an oval—something I had seen Micah do over and over every time he was in his grandfather's swing in Texas!

I burst into tears, wailing as I cried out Micah's name. It was him—it HAD to be!

Anna just about lost it, too! "I can't believe what I'm seeing, even though I'm standing here looking at it!" she cried. She took the bottles of water out of my hands, placed them on the table nearby, and deliberately wrapped me in her arms.

Intuitively, she knew I was on the brink of complete collapse. She stood there holding me tightly as I continued a deep, guttural wailing. Every cell in my body knew my son was on that swing— something only a mother could recognize—despite his invisibility.

The swing continued its elliptical movement as Anna gently ushered me away from the window and over to the couch. She continued holding me tightly in her arms as I curled into a fetal position, nestled against her body.

It was May 17, Micah's thirty-second birthday.

38

Micah Pays a Visit

(August 2011)

Unexpectedly, on June 7, 2011—my third wedding anniversary—ten weeks after Micah's death and two weeks short of his ninety-first birthday, my father silently, peacefully slipped away in his sleep. I did not get to talk to him or see him before he died, and emotionally I was crushed.

From a more stoic perspective, I had done the death drill enough times that despite my pain, I was able to plan and make my way through my father's funeral. Soon after, I started the process of clearing out sixty years of "stuff" from his house and workshop.

It is total hell to be an only child and the last person standing. By the end of June, I felt exhausted and beaten down. How I put one foot in front of the other is something only God can answer.

I returned to North Carolina just in time to finish renovations on our mountain house before guests would begin arriving in early July. The renovations had been the topic of the last real conversation I had had with my father. I could see the image of him on his last visit there—his silhouette as he sat on the deck, overlooking Grandfather Mountain and sipping Gentleman Jack in his red checkered shirt and warm wool pants.

On the night of July 3, around ten o'clock, I let Harmony out and went outside with her to keep a watchful eye on her—bears wandering the woods nearby are common. I remained on the asphalt driveway while she sniffed and meandered around the front and side yards.

Suddenly—and quite surprisingly, I might add—I found myself on the ground in excruciating pain, trying to lift myself off the edge of the asphalt where it met the grass. What had just happened? Had someone knocked me down? If so, who? Better yet, why? Did anyone see me as I picked myself up off the ground? I felt off-kilter, fuzzy, and somewhat disoriented, but I managed to call Harmony to come inside.

As I walked toward the house, I could feel sharp pain in my head. I tidied up the kitchen, prepared the coffee pot so that all the early risers had to do was push the "on" button, and prepared for bed. I still felt confused as I lay my head down on the pillow to sleep.

The next morning, I was the last person to awaken. With a house full of guests and more arriving that morning, I could not believe I had overslept. I rushed to get up, got dressed, and made it to the kitchen just as the new guests were walking in. What had happened to me? I shook it off for now.

My friend Barbara noticed a knot on my forehead and scrape marks on my left shoulder and left knee. I mentioned what had happened the night before, and after a brief examination, she said she believed I had a concussion. Based on the bruising and strawberry markings on my body, I had collapsed on my left side, hitting my head on the asphalt as my body dropped. The question was why.

Once back in Charlotte, I underwent extensive heart and brain testing, including treadmill, stress, tilt-table, and 24-hour heart-monitor tests for a month. I needed to go back to Texas to finish clearing out my father's house and shop, but clearly, I could go nowhere far until the test results were back. So while I waited, I went to our beach condo at Litchfield near Pawleys Island, South Carolina, to rest and recuperate.

I love the ocean—the sand, the smells, the sounds, and the tide that moves in synchrony with the moon. Somehow, I am at perfect peace when I am on or at the ocean; I seem to become one with it. And given that our bodies are about 60 percent water, who's to say I don't move with the tide when I'm there?

I found myself very relaxed, lying on the couch with the sliding doors open so I could hear and smell the ocean. I felt as if I were literally on the beach, even though I was two floors up.

It was there—on the teal, blue, yellow, and white 1980s beach-motif sofa—that I fell into the deepest sleep I had had in a very long time.

Suddenly, it seemed that crowds were gathered all around me, everywhere as far as the eye could see. Streets were lined with anxious onlookers jumping up and down, hollering, and holding homemade posters, like groupies awaiting the arrival of a limo carrying their favorite rock star. Police maintained barricades and did their best to keep order.

When the car arrived, the sea of people parted to let it pass and then swarmed behind, closing the gap and following it as it moved to the red carpet–lined pathway to an entrance into a hotel-like building. I had never seen so many people. Who were they? Why were they there? Who were they going bonkers over?

The car stopped at least half a block short of the red-carpet entrance. The right back door opened, and a tall, lean man with dark sunglasses, wearing a gray, tight-fitting T-shirt, skinny blue jeans, and white shell-toed shoes stepped out of the limo into the crowd. The high shrill of female voices could be heard above the roar of the rest of the crowd.

I watched from a window at least three stories above the action. I felt as though I were part of the activity but that at the same time, I was an observer of it. And then realization spread throughout my body: it became clear to me that the rock star below was my son, Micah!

He had returned from death, making a grand entrance full of pomp and circumstance and surrounded by everyone he had ever met or come in contact with—all of whom were ecstatic to see him, as if he had been away on vacation. Somehow, they knew he would be returning, and unbeknownst to me, someone had planned a major celebration for this event. People were running up to him, hugging him, kissing him, and holding onto him for fear he would leave again. He literally had to push people away from him to make his way through the crowd.

Still, I watched from above. Why was he here? Why hadn't I known? Did he love me as he appeared to love his friends? What about his show of affection to total strangers? Why wasn't I invited to this event?

As I watched him move, charismatically maneuvering through the crowds, I noticed that when *he* was ready, a few close friends and family members somehow knew to join him inside, behind the ornate double doors of the building. Those who were uninvited knew not to push, and once Micah moved inside, the crowds took about thirty minutes to disperse.

Once everyone had disappeared from sight, I decided to get a closer look at what was happening. I progressed down the red carpet, opened the heavy ornate doors, and proceeded inside. A type of cocktail party event was going on, with people standing around chatting and eating. I didn't know most of the people I saw. I scanned the room for Micah, but he was nowhere to be found.

I heard noise coming from a stairway that led downstairs. Slowly, I took each step, one at the time, down into a basement-like game room. I scanned the area, and through the group of people standing around—some talking, some eating, some drinking, and others playing pool—my eyes caught Micah's big brown eyes at the same time his caught mine.

My heart raced. I felt like an intruder. I froze on the next-to-last step, watching him as he carefully ran the table, cigarette hanging from his mouth. He looked up at me and nodded in the affirmative. Slowly, I made my way down the next two steps and then became immobilized as I checked the air to determine whether or not I was welcome.

Why did he not drop everything and run over to hug me as soon as he saw me? Why did I feel so apprehensive? As these questions floated through my head, he slowly began to move toward me, at which time I lifted my right foot to move also. Our gaze was deep, eye to eye. The fun I'd been watching him have seemed to stop the closer we got to one another. Standing face-to-face, I told him I loved him very much.

He looked at me and said, "I love you, too. It's good to see you," he continued, as he loosely hugged me.

I felt I had placed a damper on the party and that he was being cordial in hugging me and telling me he loved me; deep inside I sensed he was full of anger and somewhat confused about how he really felt toward me.

Tears coursed down my cheeks as I opened my eyes. Two hours had passed, according to the clock on the wall. Had I traveled somewhere? Had I had a dream? Had my son returned to tell everyone he was doing OK? Why did I feel he still believed I didn't love him?

My heart ached and tears continued to flow. *Time*, I heard; *it will just take time. . . .*

39

The Pocket Watch

(September 2011)

I was getting antsy and anxious about getting back to Texas to tackle the work I had ahead of me. Why? Partly, I believe, to stay busy, and partly because there was no one else to do it—legally or physically. After wearing a heart monitor for a month, I had the follow-up appointment with the cardiologist to get test results, and happily, nothing was wrong.

"All tests were normal," he beamed, as he gave me the statistics on how many people black out for no reason and no known cause. He cleared me to go back to my tasks in Texas and let me know he felt that my life events over the past few months would have taken Goliath down. He assured me that he would always be there if anything showed up. I thanked him and laughingly said I hoped never to see him again—no offense!

The magnitude of the work in Texas was daunting. To my surprise, I was honored by old high school friends who came out of the woodwork to help me. We had not seen one another since graduating in 1974, but being with them actually turned out to be fun and cathartic. My sentinel, Kay, always remained by my side.

I knew I had to take care of myself emotionally and physically during the weeks and months of work ahead of me, so on occasion, I would take a day off for EFT (Emotional Freedom Technique) sessions, lunch, shopping in the city, or sessions with other healers. I had not seen Petrene since March, when Micah passed, so I decided to spend an afternoon with her to "play"—but more to allow her to assess where I was in my process of healing from my immense losses.

She asked how I felt about doing a rebirthing session. My body shivered in anticipation at the thought of such nurturing care, and I said, "Let's begin!" I spent four hours with her in this process, and when we ended the session, I felt a bit rubber-legged, so I sat down on the floor. Petrene took a seat in a chair facing me.

She broke the silence saying, "Your son is here. He has something to say to you." I was not surprised, because as soon as she began speaking, I picked up on him psychically. She told me he was very angry. "Yes, he is," I affirmed.

As she spoke, I could see images of him. He was wearing a red and gray plaid long-sleeved shirt with a pocket on the left side. His face was drawn and mean. It was the face of someone carrying deep hurt and pain. I could sense and feel the intensity of his anger, including the part he held toward me.

The images I saw were from a time when he was in a very bad place. It was after Michael had left and Micah had gone AWOL from Hargrave. Micah was living in Texas with my parents—the safest place for him at that time. Looking back, I could see his deep hurt, pain, and feelings of unworthiness, fear, and confusion; all of these images and emotions showered me in less than a second.

Petrene continued sharing the information she was receiving and told me he had a favor to ask of me. Now that was the Micah I knew: mad and pissed off at me but still asking me for something! Petrene let me know I did not have to honor his request, but somehow, I felt I wanted to—not out of guilt but out of curiosity about the communication happening between the world he was in and the world I was in, and for the possible healing it could provide. If there were anything I could do to help him where he was, I certainly wanted to.

Once I agreed, he instantaneously and telepathically showed Petrene a pocket watch hanging out of the left pocket of the shirt he had on. As Petrene described what she saw, I told her I could see the same thing—and I knew exactly what it was! I told her he had stolen a pocket watch from his paternal grandfather when he was about the age of the image he was showing us!

As I spoke those words, both of us could feel the air of immense anger, hurt, and pain emanating from him. The feeling penetrated both of us. Amazing! What an experience! Though unhealed on this side of the veil, the negative feelings somehow seemed to be getting worked out on the other.

I asked what my role in this was and what the favor Micah wanted was. She suggested I buy a pocket watch, put it on the windowsill in the light, and leave it there for about three weeks. Once those words were spoken, the air of anger disappeared and the room cleared. Then, rather lackadaisically and off-the-cuff, as the essence of Micah was departing, he indicated to Petrene, "Oh, by the way, tell my mom thank you for my name."

She looked at me quizzically on that one and said, "He said to thank you for his name."

"Micah Aaron Matthew Felcman. I selected his names from the Bible." Still sitting on the floor, I looked up at Petrene and exclaimed, "That was HUGE!"

"Very!" she said, with strong emotion in her voice.

We drank a cup of tea together, smiling and shaking our heads at the power of the experience we had just shared, before I made the hour-long drive back to my parents' house to resume my duties. During the drive, I revisited what had happened over and over—enough to make my drive seem like ten minutes rather than sixty.

I drove directly to Wal-Mart in Liberty, where I found the one and only pocket watch in the store! It was on a chain, and it was silver with a white face and Roman numerals. Magically, it cost nine dollars (I say magically because nine is symbolic of a triple trinity). I recalled that Micah's grandfather's watch had also been silver with a white face! My being radiated as I held the box in my hands and paid for the watch—and like a pregnant woman en route to the hospital to deliver, I lost no time getting to my parents' house. I had no idea what to expect, so I decided to have no expectations—just put the watch on the windowsill in the kitchen, in the light, and would let happen whatever was in God's plan to happen.

When I left Texas in mid-November, the watch remained in the light on the windowsill.

40

Thank You

(December 2011)

I spent Thanksgiving at Enchantment Resort, nestled tightly in Boynton Canyon in the healing energy of Sedona, Arizona. Christmas and New Year's were spent in the warm waters of the Caribbean on my first cruise. It was impossible for me to remain in Charlotte over the holidays the first year after Micah's death. After all, for thirty-two years, the Thanksgiving turkey and Christmas festivities had been done mainly for him. Intuitively, I knew that I would create new traditions, but I simply was not ready yet.

One day, back in Charlotte between trips, I was doing laundry. As I turned away from the washer and dryer, arms loaded with folded towels to put away, the air suddenly felt so thick that I felt as if I were walking right through something. Immediately, I realized it was Micah; I recognized and felt his essence. As I did, I saw an image of the pocket watch and clairaudiently heard him loudly say, "Thank you!"

In the moment he was "there," I could feel he was in a much better place, the intensity of his anger no longer present. He seemed genuinely thankful and simply wanted me to know. I felt as if he were in a process of healing the things he had not done while incarnate, and as a mother, I felt comforted.

I smiled softly and went about putting the towels away.

41

The Help

(February 21, 2012)

In early February, I hosted a healing circle at my townhouse, which had been the venue for healing events for many years. Traditionally, our circle of six to eight ladies met once a month for one-and-a-half to two hours, enjoying social time for the first thirty minutes of the gathering and then doing energy healing for one another during the rest of the time.

We held these circles over an extended lunch hour, so those who needed to get back to work were free to leave when they needed to, while those who had a bit of extra time would sometimes hang back and continue the social element of the circle. All cell phones went into the off position upon entrance.

On this particular day, as ladies were arriving, we noticed a helicopter flying low overhead, making big circles around the town house and the surrounding area. The roar and whir of the blades was very loud, like what one might imagine the onset of an aerial military invasion to sound like. Despite the disturbance, we continued our gathering, invoking the silence that normally began our healing session.

Our focus was razor-sharp despite the noise of the now multiple helicopters outside. Each one of us took our turn on the table while the others deliberately and mindfully administered and balanced the energy body of the person on the table. Eventually, the helicopters vanished into the distance.

We went over our scheduled time, so once the last person was off the table, everyone left quickly—except for Joyce and me. I was pouring a glass of lemonade while Joyce checked her voice mail, when suddenly, I heard her gutturally scream, "No, no, no!" She fell in a heap on the floor, tears everywhere.

My immediate feeling was that something severe had happened to one of her children, but I could get no response from her in her traumatized state. So I held her tightly as she cried, and I helped get her to the closest chair. Once she caught her breath, she told me that her nephew, Curtis, who lived right around the corner from the townhouse, had crashed into a tree one block from home and had died instantly!

"Oh my God!" came out of my mouth, as my mind's eye saw exactly what had happened. How did I know this young man had had a struggle with drugs? How did I know he had gone out to get drugs and was in a hurry to get home before anyone knew he had left? How did I know? Why did I know?

In the moments of chaos, confusion, and hurt that followed, I realized that the helicopter flyover was because of this accident. As I held my friend in her distress, I felt compelled to call out to Micah to help Curtis's soul as it was entering the other side. I cried out and pleaded to Micah, stating that he knew what it was like to deal with drug addiction and asking him to please help. "We need your help!" I cried. "Please help us NOW!" I commanded into the invisible space above the chair where I still held Joyce tightly.

All I knew to do was pray—pray for her nephew, pray for her and her family, and pray for Micah where he was. My prayers were said aloud and appeared to bring comfort to Joyce.

For me, reliving the intense trauma and death of Joyce's nephew was far too close to home not to have an emotional impact on me. It had been only eleven months since I'd gone through the same trauma, and despite all the healing I thought I had done, I was worse off than I'd realized.

That night I researched retreats in the area and decided to leave the next morning for Well of Mercy, a spiritual retreat run by the Sisters of Mercy convent. When I made the reservation, I had no idea how long I would stay, but I intuitively felt three days would be helpful for my soul. The location—Harmony, North Carolina—was about two hours north and east of Charlotte.

I got up the next morning and struck out for Harmony. Literally and figuratively, harmony was exactly what I needed to bring balance back to my being after the salt that had been poured directly on my wound the day before and that had reignited my pain. I got lost in the soft sounds of the music I listened to as I drove north on Interstate 85.

Then, about thirty minutes out of Harmony and less than twenty-four hours since the accident—coming in loud and clear from my left side and passing over me to the right—I heard, "Ma! Ma! I did all I could!" in Micah's tone of voice, as if he were sitting right beside me in the car. The intonation was firm and deliberate, almost as if he were shouting to make certain that I could hear him.

Immediately, I felt he was letting me know there were limits to what he *could* do but that he had done what he was *allowed* to do. What the "help" was, I have no idea. As this realization filled my being, I had to pull the car over to the side of the road and sob. My body shook and shuddered uncontrollably as tears flowed.

In less than twenty-four hours, my son, who had crossed over eleven months earlier, had responded to my desperate plea to help another soul who, like him, had died suddenly as a result of his struggle with drug addiction. I marveled at the beauty of this event, crying softly until I was composed enough to continue my journey.

Another thirty minutes and I was "off the grid," pulling into Well of Mercy. I checked in, put my bags in my room, and headed outside to be in the fresh air. I meandered down the hill to a stream, and to my surprise, I found a trail to wander off into the woods to be close to nature. I was still reeling and wanted to ground in nature to reflect on what had just happened.

I had not traveled far into the woods when I looked up and saw, directly in front of me, a crucifix nailed on a tree to my left! I stopped dead in my tracks, tears flowing like a hard three-day rain making its way down a mountain, following the path of least resistance.

I stood there, facing the crucifix affixed to the large pin oak tree, in awe of God's Divinity. My friend's nephew, Curtis, had lost his life hitting an oak tree, and my son was there to "help" from beyond the veil. The tree before me was God's message and comfort that both of them were OK and in His hands.

42

Kitchen Conversation

(April 2012)

Since Micah's passing on March 29, 2011, a new tradition of mine has been to make an altar by placing one or two of his 8" x 10" head shots or photographs with his children on the dining room table, along with numerous varieties of white flowers. One might say this is truly an area of extravagance for me, as I love flowers and this occasion gives me permission to indulge. I love stargazer lilies, white roses, carnations, daisies, calla lilies—you name it, and they are probably on the dining table in our house at this time of year. I keep white flowers out until May 17, when I shift to vibrant, loud colors in celebration of Micah's birth.

I place the white flowers on the table at approximately 4:00 a.m. (EST) on the morning of March 29, the time of his death in 2011. I awaken early, say prayers, and do a meditation in honor of his life and journey with me. The table is beautiful, and the aroma of flowers permeates every nook and cranny of the house.

One afternoon during the second week of April, 2012, I decided to water the flowers, trim them, remove dead flowers and leaves, and rearrange the vases as necessary. I carried one or two vases of flowers from the dining room to the kitchen at a time, gently placing them near the sink. My mind was occupied with the flower-refreshing project, and my hands were busy pulling dead leaves, snapping off dead or wilted flowers, and cutting rotten stems—when suddenly, I realized Micah was sitting on the kitchen counter immediately to my left, observing my activities.

When he realized I was aware of his presence, he began telepathically communicating with me. What a kick! It was as though we were talking to each other—except our mouths never opened!

I had refreshed the two vases of flowers and began walking back to the dining table. As I did, he "floated" right beside me, as if he were walking with me. He telepathically showed me the bead that had dropped onto the tile floor back in April 2011. I stopped dead in my tracks, and speaking to the "air" beside me, I exclaimed, "I knew it was you!"

He continued with his messaging, and interestingly, he was able to evoke feelings in me as he communicated. It was as if he were showing me what it felt like for him—which really got my attention. As he continued to project, doing an almost complete replay of the bead incident, he indicated to me that he was *always right there with us.* He communicated how emotionally painful and deeply hurtful it was to him when we didn't know he was there and couldn't see him—and how excruciatingly traumatic it was for him to be so close to his children but at the same time so far away.

Somewhat in a stupor, I positioned the flower vases on the dining table, leaning over to pick up two more and head back to the kitchen. His presence stayed by my side. Tears began flowing down my cheeks as I reflected on how hard and how long I had tried everything known to humankind to help him heal his addiction, to live as an example, and to show him a different way.

I felt he could read my mind because, as my body became laden with a heavy sadness, he abruptly interjected, telling me not to go there in my thoughts. Somehow, he was able to quickly dissipate and remove the feeling I was experiencing. He placed his etheric arms around me and softly said, "Mom, always remember: every soul is responsible for its own journey and affects every other being on Earth and elsewhere. You have no idea how far things you do go on this side. View another's journey with respect and honor—not fear, anger, or pity. Few realize that sadness and pity are disrespectful to the soul."

The tone of his communication and the wisdom he showed brought a peaceful smile to my face and gentle warmth to my being. As his essence disappeared, I looked skyward with thanks and gratitude for the healing and understanding he was receiving in what I will call his soul's purification and Life Review—and for his desire to communicate his newfound wisdom to me on this side of the veil. It felt as if he were letting me know that where he was, he was getting all I had tried to teach him and help him with during our incarnate journey together!

Our caduceus of life had just made another touch point. Both of us were healing.

43

Robin Tekwelus Youngblood

(October 2012)

In the early evening of October 22, 2012, I heard the phone ringing inside and frantically rushed into the house from the garage, arms loaded with groceries and dropping items as I did my best to place the bags on the counter and answer the phone at the same time. The voice on the other end was that of my friend, Debbie P.

Debbie's voice is soft and pleasant to listen to. Although we don't hang out a lot, our common connection is our work with Hospice Pet Therapy, which is where we met. Through joint visits, continuing education, and other basic girl stuff, we have grown to know each other better.

Her voice sounded tired but overloaded with excitement as she told me about a Native American grandmother named Robin Tekwelus Youngblood, who travels the globe and just happened to be at Sacred Grove Retreat Center in Gold Hill, North Carolina. Debbie had spent time with Robin and said she had no clue why she felt so strongly about telling me of Robin—but that was the purpose of her call.

I thanked her for thinking of me, began cooking dinner, and proceeded to put the remaining groceries away.

After dinner, during my evening bath, something told me I needed to contact Robin Youngblood—that Debbie was a messenger and I really needed to pay attention. I decided I would ring this woman first thing next morning. Why? I wasn't completely sure, but I knew the gentle nudge of Divine Guidance. I felt something was unresolved related to my Native American past life and that it was a possible connection to the new "language" uncorked in me on May 17, 2012—Micah's thirty-third birthday. Although I wasn't certain what it was, the sounds, tones, and expressions coming through my voice and throat felt like a form of communication. Rock said I spoke it in my sleep at times.

Fortunately, when I phoned Sacred Grove the next morning, I was delighted to learn there was one space left for a one-on-one session with Robin at two o'clock on the 24th. Now I was really getting excited. I knew "something" would be taught or revealed, and I could hardly wait to see what that was and how it would unfold.

I decided to leave at noon on the twenty-fourth, partly because I was excited and partly because I didn't know exactly where I was going and didn't want to get lost or be late. The drive was at least an hour and a half from my home. I arrived on time, found a place to park, got out of the car, and intuitively walked right up to Robin, who was sitting under a tree.

Wisdom radiated from her face. Our eyes met, and our souls touched and intertwined in seconds as she stood up, extending her arms to embrace me as though we were longtime friends. Immediately, I felt comforted by her genuineness. We walked shoulder to shoulder through the woods to the yurt, a circular tent of skins stretched over a pole frame built up on a wooden floor. She burned sage; laid out a flute, drum, rattles, and crystals; and pulled the skins down over the windows. She asked that I sit directly across from her, cross-legged on the sacred blanket.

"Mindy, why are you here?" she asked piercingly.

"I'm not sure," I replied sheepishly, as I tried to gather my thoughts and get my act together.

"Yes, you do," she said gently. "Sit quietly for a moment and then tell me."

Different kinds of things were running through my mind when almost uncontrollably, I blurted out, "Is there a connection to my Native American past life and the language that is coming from me now?"

She asked if I could speak this language to her, and I explained I had never done it on command, but I believed I could now because I could feel it bubbling up in my body as she asked the question. Sure enough, here it came.

She looked at me with great kindness and told me it was not a Native American dialect but a spiritual language we all know and understand on a soul level. It made sense to me, especially since it had started on what would have been my son's thirty-third birthday. I felt it was just another way of communication beyond what we know and understand on this side of the veil. OK, whew! That was out of the way—so now what?

"Tell me about your son, Mindy," she stated.

I proceeded to tell her everything I could recall about him, including all the details of the Native American past life the two of us had shared as medicine men. I explained how we had lost our tribe to a disease that we could not treat, and I told her about the sadness, guilt, and responsibility we had carried over into this life.

Micah had sought to remedy his guilt and sadness through the use of drugs, ultimately leading to addiction. As a result, I had sought new ways of healing addiction, but I learned quickly that I cannot be responsible for the outcome of another's actions. For me this was the purpose of my awareness of the Native American life: so I could heal and release the cellular memory of feeling responsible for the lives of my tribe.

The sadness and heaviness seemed to be with me like a wet blanket and intensified in this life when I visited Boynton Canyon in Sedona, Arizona, in 2011. While hiking behind the hotel, I found four crosses erected in the four directions, colored white, green, black, and yellow. As I stood in the center of them, I could see and feel masses of Native American men, women, and children walking on a path—the Trail of Tears. I felt the intensity of the loss of a race, the despondency, sadness, and heaviness of a people who were seriously ill and dying and who were displaced from everything they knew.

I connected our previous Native American life to this life and had done all I could to heal that life in this one. For Micah, it seemed he took a darker path in this life despite his awareness of the Native American life and what he was working out in this life. Just as we have no "cure" for drug addiction today, in the Native American life, there was no "cure" for the bubonic plague and other diseases brought into this country by the white race. In obvious ways, he was still punishing himself in this life for the losses in the Native American life.

Robin listened quietly and intently, paying attention to each word out of my mouth and the feeling emanating from my body as I spoke. "Are you ready and are you willing to forgive the Europeans who brought these diseases to this land?" she asked.

"Yes, yes, I am . . . and I don't know how I know this, but Micah is, too," I managed to utter through the mass of tears that welled up in my eyes.

No sooner had the words come out of my mouth than I felt the tightness in my body begin to relax. "Oh my God! Have I been holding resentment and anger inside of me today for people I am not conscious of and who caused my tribe to die in another life?" I asked aloud.

"Yes, you have, and so has your son," Robin responded. "I want you to feel the space that is now opened up inside you, and I want you to fill the space by breathing pure, unconditional love into those cells. I also want you to surround the Europeans who brought the plagues into this land with the same unconditional love," she directed.

I was awed and amazed at how much this unseen blanket of sadness and heaviness that had clouded much of my life since early childhood was lifted. I felt lighter, and so did the air around me. Wow!

I was overwhelmed and elated, all at the same time, but I suddenly began to feel tired. I felt we were just about finished when Robin said, "Wait a minute; we are being led to do a shamanic journey. There is something else. . . ."

"Please lie down on the floor and make yourself comfortable. There is an angelic presence that has shown up to my right, near the top of your head. I will beat the drum and speak as guided. Take three deep cleansing breaths, and do not forget to call in your guide, who will accompany you on this journey," she instructed as she began a slow, rhythmic beat of the drum.

As I lay there, my relaxed body sinking into the floor, I allowed my mind to wander, feeling as though I was becoming one with the floor. In this deeply relaxed state, much to my surprise, to my right, my maternal grandmother, Minnie, showed up as my guide. *What? I was expecting something super-cosmic!* my mind exclaimed. *Why are you here?*

Now my mind was in a game of tug-of-war, and I knew my job was to quiet it. But I was having serious difficulty. *Minnie died on May 17, 1977, between 5:00 and 5:30 a.m. (CST), and Micah was born two years later on the same day, at 5:10 a.m. (CST).* Once my mind remembered that connection, I returned to my relaxed state, accepting that my grandmother was not going anywhere. My mind quieted and the battle ceased.

It seemed as though I were flying low over a desertlike landmass when I heard Robin ask me if I had had a long-ago life in the Middle East. "Maybe," I said.

The place below me held nothing for me. So, as if I were flying over a large map, I made a forty-five-degree diagonal left turn and zoomed directly to Beijing, China. "Oh my God, here we go," I said quietly to myself as my body and being reverberated with full recall of color, smell, clothing, people, sounds, voices, and my physical collapse at the last gate of the Forbidden City.

I flashed back to March 2007, when I was in Beijing working for Bank of America on the China Construction Bank project. On one of our few days off, our team decided to visit the Imperial Palace and the Forbidden City. The place was packed so tightly with tourists that it was hard for our group to stay together without concentrated effort. We did a great job of it until we approached the last gate prior to entering the main courtyard of the palace.

For some unknown reason and out of nowhere, I collapsed to the ground as though I had been knocked down by an invisible force. I began sobbing. It was as if I'd become a rag doll, pushed and trampled by the crowds separating me from my group. I had no wherewithal to right myself. While on the ground, literally at the feet of anxious tourists, I felt unmitigated resistance to going any farther into the compound. I felt I had been there before, and I sensed something terrible had happened to me there.

My physical body shuddered in panic and deep fear as I lay on the ground, curled in a fetal position and pushed to the far right of the walkway by the irritated tourists. I was frozen and in shock. What had happened? What was going on with me? I knew I was in 2007, but I felt something else permeate my body from another time-space.

I felt someone touch me gently but firmly on my upper arm. I looked up and it was Scott, one of the members of our group. His voice brought me back to the present as he lifted me up off the ground and helped me find my footing. He took tissues out of his pocket to wipe smeared mascara off my face, and he asked, "What happened?"

"I don't know," I said, as I did my best to act cool.

He held onto my arm as we proceeded through the crowds to the courtyard, where the rest of the group was waiting under a tree. They apologized for not noticing sooner that I was missing, and when they realized my emotional state, they encircled me like sentinels for the remainder of the tour. I was thankful and grateful to them, but certain parts of the palace grounds caused my heart to race.

As we walked, we were appalled to see a Starbucks in the courtyard at the end of the tour, but we decided to meander through the bookstore that was attached to it. Immediately, I was drawn to a book written in Chinese. I thumbed through it, unable to read anything, but I did notice pictures like ones my grandmother Minnie had handed down to me. Naturally, I had to buy the book. My body slowly returned to a more normal state of being. We hailed a taxi and headed back to our hotel.

I knew this incident had meaning for me, but I never knew why or what until five and a half years later—in the yurt at Sacred Grove Retreat Center in Gold Hill, North Carolina, in October 2012 on this second past-life journey with Robin. She continued beating the drum rhythmically while guiding me to go back to March 2007 and step into the past life that had been brought forward to me during my time in Beijing.

This time there were no crowds or tourists. The palace grounds were as they were when I lived there. There were workers but no crowds. As I walked through the last gate, I meandered toward the left of the courtyard. There were two areas of single rooms, one for the concubines and one for the maidens—the workers of the palace. "Look at yourself. What do you see?" Robin queried.

I saw myself curled up on the floor in the upper right-hand corner of the small rectangular room. I was facing the wall, and my head was on the floor. There was a small table with low legs about halfway down the wall, a small light to my back, and a door that seemed far away and locked. I felt I couldn't move, as though I were anesthetized.

"Feel where you are; feel your body and tell me what is happening," Robin directed.

"I am a concubine. I am in an opium den. I am used for the pleasure of others, and I am kept drugged. I cannot get up," I managed to say. The feeling was just like what I had felt in 2007 when I collapsed!

"Whose concubine are you?" Robin asked.

"The emperor's or his son, maybe both," I uttered.

"Your son in this life was the emperor's son in the Chinese life, and he kept you addicted to opiates for his personal pleasure. Your grandmother in this life was the empress in the Chinese life and turned a blind eye to what the men did during that era," Robin stated with conviction.

As I lay on the floor of the yurt, I could feel these truths energizing my body. Now I understood why my grandmother had showed up as a guide. Still, my mind had not yet grasped all of what I had just experienced—so I lay there, tears gently rolling down my cheeks, as I asked God to help me integrate, heal, and clear all residue of this terrible life experience.

"Robin, you will not believe this, but I have framed pictures of a Chinese emperor and empress—the only things I got from my grandmother when she passed—hanging in the entryway of my town house. Also, on the sofa in the TV room, I have two opium-den pillows that I was fascinated by and bought when I lived in Singapore in the early eighties. And on top of that, the Chinese book I bought in 2007 has images of the Chinese emperor and empress that are identical to those hanging in my house!" I said in a flabbergasted voice as I pieced things together.

Robin asked if I felt ready to finish the journey. This experience was *big*, and she wanted me to seal the healing that had occurred.

"Yes, I am ready. I am thankful and grateful to you, to the angels, to my grandmother, and to the others who showed up to help me," I replied.

Again, she asked me to open and deeply breathe Divine Unconditional Love into my being. She asked if I were willing to become a vessel large enough to hold the love that it would take to heal addiction. I answered, "Oh my God, yes! Yes!"

In that moment, I realized that Micah was deep in his Life Review on the other side of the veil and that it was critical for both of us to heal and clear the karma of the Chinese life we had shared. He had designed his current life of addiction as a way to treat himself as he had once treated another in order to balance out his own soul's evolution. All anger, hurt, pain, repression, sadness, heaviness, low self-esteem, guilt, and other negative emotions were removed through multiple dimensions and time-space. We were healing negativity and emotional damage from six centuries prior!

I remained awestruck for several days about the nature of the life journeys my son and I had previously shared and about the profound healing of these two past lives. God has promised us life everlasting, and my experience validates that promise. This experience helped me to further realize that all healing is possible, no matter what the infirmity or what the nature of its roots may be.

In this life, Micah had the opportunity to heal, but for some reason, he did not. As soon as he crossed over, he had no choice but to see where he might have chosen differently, and it seems he immediately embarked on the healing journey I had hoped we would have in this life.

As I feel God smiling down on me, I see that Micah and I received every bit of the healing we both needed once we relinquished our will to "Thy will." We cannot miss our lessons, and despite what we might desire for a loved one, ultimately, the journey is between the soul of the loved one and God. We are simply actors in the play of the journey of life, here to support others on their path—not to take the journey they have chosen away from them or dictate how it should be lived.

Once we realize this and begin living our lives accordingly, we can eradicate pain and suffering, and the human race can evolve into one with no illness.

44

T-Shirt Quilts

(Second week of November 2012)

In 2011, the person for whom I had traditionally erected a Christmas tree for thirty-two years was no longer physically present, making the holidays something I could not physically or emotionally endure. But in 2012, I felt I wanted to decorate the house early, plan parties, and really get into the spirit of the season. Little did I know how "spirited" the season would become!

In the process of getting the house ready, I entered a closet that I primarily use for off-season storage of clothing. While rummaging around in there, I found a few large bags full of Micah's T-shirts that I had been saving until the time was right to make quilts out of them for his children. I pulled the large, heavy, black forty-gallon bags from the shelf, sensing that now was the time.

As I gently opened the bags, the smell of my son that was embedded in the clothing caught me off guard. *Am I really ready for this?* I missed him so. The moment of sadness that poured through me seemed to allow me to acknowledge my pain, bathe myself in his fragrance, and move on with a strength that confirmed that the time was right.

I laid out all the T-shirts in order to know what size quilt I could make for the children. I determined that there were enough for two twin-sized quilts, and I proceeded to scoop the shirts up to take them to wash. The aroma of my son would be gone forever now.

I had contacted a quilting company to stitch the T-shirts together, but first I had to lay them out in the order I wanted, numbering each piece. As these newly washed T-shirts were laid out on my living room floor, I could feel and sense a gentle guidance as to which child was to get which shirt and where it was supposed to go!

I was specifically guided to have each of their names embroidered over the left pocket. Skylar's name would go on a red T-shirt, and Parker's name would go on a black one. The script was to read "SKYLAR, with love, Pappa" and "PARKER, with love, Pappa." I was taken aback by the specific instructions I received, and I became more fascinated at how long it took to get each quilt laid out. Once each set of instructions was in order and complete, I mailed them off with the T-shirts in hopes of getting the quilts back in time for Christmas.

One afternoon in mid-December, the postman delivered a very large box, which I knew must be the quilts. "Yes!" I exclaimed, as I maneuvered the box inside the house. I opened the box to find each quilt wrapped delicately and separately. With grandeur I unfurled each one carefully, laying them on the living room floor. Wow! I could hardly believe my eyes, seeing the transformation of Micah's T-shirts into something of deep meaning and beauty.

At about the same time my eyes started to tear, I felt a rush of information come through me, and I got a sheet of paper to begin writing:

Merry Christmas 2012
Dear Skylar and Parker,

I asked Grannie to make a quilt out of my old T-shirts so each night when you lie down to sleep, you may cover yourself and know that I am there.

When you look at the quilt, see how many things you can learn about me. Can you tell my favorite color? Some of the places I went? Where I worked? What do you see? Can you feel my love for you?

Notice I asked Grannie to have your name put on one of my favorite shirts with a pocket—close to my heart! Can you find it?

Parker, did you notice the square with one of your names? Skylar, what about the one with the day of your birth?

Never forget how much I love you! Have a Merry Christmas, and remember to be nice to your mother. She loves you, too!

Love,
Pappa

Once my body stopped shaking and the tears stopped flowing, I copied the message on a dry sheet of paper in more legible handwriting, to enclose in the box that was sure to reach the children by Christmas.

45

Full-Court Press

(November 26–December 3, 2012)

Thanksgiving was over, and as I mentioned, I was looking forward to the Christmas holiday season this year. Rock's daughter, Lydia, was with us for Thanksgiving and was sleeping in the Friday morning after. I don't think I'd ever done this before, but I got the bug to start putting the Christmas tree up that morning.

I managed to get all of the pieces out of storage, put them together, and voilà! When Lydia woke up, there was a fancy eleven-foot artificial fir tree standing in the living room. By Sunday evening, I had dragged all the boxes of ornaments inside and started strategically placing them on the tree.

The tree is so tall that I need a ladder to reach the top, and then I'm on my tippy-toes, stretching to properly place each ornament at arm's length or trimming according to its size, color, and shape. For some reason, Harmony loves to bite at my legs when I climb up. So between her barks and playful bites and the height of the tree, decorating can be rather comical—albeit scary at the top.

This year my cousin Kay was coming from Texas to spend a long week with us. Everyone in my immediate family had passed, so for me, it felt wonderful to have any family with me at Christmas. Don't get me wrong—I have exceptional friends and Rock's family is great, but there was something special about having Kay with me this year. It brought back the excitement we had shared at Christmas when we were kids.

Monday morning, November 26, I resumed my decorating project. While atop the ladder, I felt Micah's presence. Immediately, I felt saddened that he was not here for the holidays, and I did all I could to keep myself from falling into a melancholy state through the tears that gently flowed from my eyes. I wanted to do my best to have a happy holiday, to resume life, and to enjoy decorating in a way I hadn't done in a long time. I descended the ladder and decided to run a few errands, hoping to change the energy of the feelings I was having.

An amazing series of events happened next.

The Girl

I stopped at the post office on Carmel Road to mail a couple of letters and packages. I stood in line at one of the self-service kiosks for what seemed an eternity. Frustrated, I got out of line and went to another kiosk, only to stand in line there, too—and then when it was my turn, the machine broke!

Grudgingly, I moved back to the first kiosk, now farther back in the line. While standing there, to my disbelief, I saw something that almost made me faint. The word *Micah* was tattooed on the back of the neck of the girl standing directly in front of me! I knew he had been present at the house, trying to get my attention—and if this wasn't validation, I don't know what was!

I stood there in awe, unable to talk to the girl and knowing I would certainly collapse if I uttered a word. Tears rolled again as I gently pulled my cell phone out of my purse to take a picture of this stranger's neck—a stranger who unknowingly had a powerful message for me. What were the odds of the girl having her hair pulled up, having *Micah* tattooed on her neck, and standing directly in front of me? Not to mention the timing of my moving to another machine, standing there, and then returning to the original kiosk. It was all too serendipitous not to be divine communication about my son. The message was mine, and I knew it! I felt good inside and headed home to continue decorating the tree.

The Form

On November 29, I had a new-patient appointment with Carolina Dermatology scheduled at 8:30 a.m. The receptionist asked that I go online and complete their forms, print them, and bring them with me to the appointment. Midmorning on the twenty-eighth, I sat down at my computer to complete the forms and was blindsided—taken off guard as I had never been before.

I had just begun filling out the form, typing my information on the relevant lines, when suddenly, just below the Carolina Dermatology logo, I noticed the word FELCMAN. It took a while for my mind to grasp that Felcman had nothing to do with this form—so why was it there? A cold chill ran through my body as my eyes read the following:

Child of MICAH FELCMAN
and MICHELE ORSBON is:
    i.   SKYLAR^7 FELCMAN

The font type was not familiar, nor was the manner in which the information was written—almost as if it had come from a book or an outline. My head was spinning. There had been no forewarning, no feeling of my son's presence—nothing but these words mysteriously positioned on the form.

I printed the document, not knowing whether or not the words would appear on the paper—but sure enough, they did. I snatched the paper off the printer, still staring at the top right corner, and I walked into the kitchen to show it to Rock. I didn't say a word other than to ask him to look at the top right corner and tell me what he saw. Being the logical engineer type, he said, "There's got to be an explanation for this!" By now, my body was shaking so hard I felt I was just shy of falling to the floor. *Why? Why?*

I thought someone or something was trying to reach me, but I didn't understand who or why. Up to this point, I had always been able to feel and sense the presence of my son. But this tripped me up. I was in a complete panic. What if this were a message about Skylar—some type of forewarning?

I called my daughter-in-law, and through hysterical cries, I explained what had just happened and asked if Skylar was OK. Michele assured me that both the children were absolutely fine and safe. She asked me to take a picture of the paper and text it to her, which I did. We tried to reason out how this could have happened, but she said she had never had any interactions with Charlotte Dermatology when she lived in Charlotte, and Skylar certainly had not.

In my search for help and answers, I called Anna, the logical, practical friend who had experienced the unexplainable "swing" visit with me the year before. Anna's immediate question was, "Where did the paper come from? Maybe the writing was on the paper and you just didn't realize it."

Just to double-check, I got up from my chair, went to the closet where I store office supplies, and returned to the phone saying, "Staples!" The paper in the printer was from Staples . . . how in the world could these words have gotten on a sheet of paper in a package of 500 and shown up perfectly placed on the Carolina Dermatology form? I was so shaken and confused that I couldn't function for the remainder of the day.

I felt completely disembodied, as if I were three to four feet off the ground. I left the house, and even while driving, I felt weird. Finally, around 3:30 p.m., I ate a Rusty's cheeseburger and came back down to earth.

I returned home with the courage to print out another page, just to see if the mysterious words would reappear. I sensed they would not, lest the impact of the first message be diminished. Intrepidly, I sat at my computer printing pages of the Carolina Dermatology form, and not once more in twenty pages did the words reappear!

I was satisfied that the one-time occurrence was all there would be, and somehow, it was up to me to find peace not knowing or understanding how or why it had happened.

The Dream

On Friday morning, November 30, I was driving down Pineville-Matthews Road, headed for a 9:00 a.m. coffee meeting at Caribou. Along the way, my phone jingled, alerting me to an incoming text message. Sitting at a red light, I scrolled down to read the message. Rather than feeling faint or collapsing after Wednesday's experience, I now felt "broken in," as if I could handle pretty much anything.

The text read:

> *"I had a dream about you and Micah last night. It was so real! Call me, I want to tell you all about it. XOXO Susan"*

Any fiber of doubt I had left inside me melted away. This week was different because of the frequency and the deliberateness of Micah's attempts to get my attention and the multiple ways and means of communication he was using to do it. What in the world was he working so hard to convey?

It was 3:30 that afternoon before Susan and I could talk. She said, "My dream was lucid and real. The two of you were hosting a party, and you—true to who you are—were entertaining, welcoming and making everyone comfortable. The love between you and Micah was obvious and very strong. It was a love like a deep romantic love, but also a love like that of a mother and child. Weird, but that is the way it was. He was adamant about me telling you that he was HOME and he wanted you to know that. He wants you to be happy in life, having joy like you have not experienced. He is truly HOME and wants you to be at peace. Everything is fine, and all is good."

Susan's words were intense. It was as though she had been entrusted to deliver a soul's critical message, and being the dutiful person she is, she needed me to "get it." Now I understood why he had been working so hard to reach me and why he had tried so many different ways, so frequently. This message was the most important of all since his passing, and he, too, wanted me to understand.

I felt whole again in a way I cannot describe. "Happy" is not powerful enough a word. A mother always wants to know where her child is and how that child is doing. In this case, Micah made sure I had that information.

I shared this information with Michele, my daughter-in-law, who wisely commented, "Maybe it's time for him to go on, and he wanted to let us know and say good-bye. I felt something similar when my dad died," she continued.

Yes, that's what it felt like to me, too!

The License Plate

Just when I thought there could be no more, I got a frantic phone call from Rock on Monday morning, December 3. I had just finished working out and was having coffee with my dear friend and sister, Carol Ann. I excused myself to take the call.

Rock's words were: "This is getting fucking freaky! I am driving to work and the license plate on the car in front of me reads 'Micahman'! Of all the damn cars on the road, *this* one is in front of me! What are the odds of that?"

I laughed. Despite Rock's frantic, foul language, I could feel Micah smiling through the phone—and so could Rock.

As if that weren't enough, Anna called for something else, and when I shared this story with her, she said, astonished, "Oh my God! I've seen that car three times this week!"

I smiled warmly, absorbing it all and marveling at the efforts of my discarnate son. There was no way his message was not going to get through.

The events of this ten-day period were intense and deliberate. The love I knew we had between us in our physical lives had been hidden by the illusion of addiction, and he wanted me to know that he knew and understood that the bond of love that existed between us never ends. He was about to be "erased," so to speak, so he could go on to God's next plan for him—but under no circumstances did he want to go on without letting me know this love. His last words to me in his incarnate, drug-addicted life were that he didn't believe I loved him. I knew I was dealing with the drug, not my son, and I knew that someday we would be made whole again.

That occurred for both of us over these ten days.

46

12-12-12

For many, 12-12-12 marked a "mysterious" time not unlike Y2K at the end of the year 1999. The number 12 has great significance in many cultures: in Western tradition, it is commonly associated with completeness and is viewed as a perfect and harmonious unit. It is used in religion, to tell the time of day, and in mythology—there are 12 apostles, 12 months, 12 hours, and 12 major Greek and Roman gods.

However, for me the date was no more than a series of numbers, like 6-6-66, when I had a terrible experience at the dentist's office. For whatever reason, on that date so many years before, no matter what Dr. Miller tried to do to deaden my little nine-year-old mouth, nothing seemed to work. I was so panic-stricken that the medication couldn't take effect. The fear I experienced increased my metabolism enough to impede the numbing effect of the medication—a condition that often happens with dental procedures today. The experience is one I have never forgotten.

Likewise, the experience I had on December 12, 2012, is one I'm unlikely ever to forget.

On that day, I decided to participate in a day of community activities, including meditation, drumming, toning, and eating with seventy-five others who showed up for the same purpose at Sacred Grove Retreat Center. The event was held during the middle of the week, making it very attractive and *different* for me—anything to break up my normal routine! It was a typical December day in the mid-Atlantic region of the United States: cool to cold, dampish, and with a gray to sometimes bright-blue sky.

Our day began outside in a large circle—setting individual intentions and saying silent prayers and blessings for the Earth, our loved ones, and ourselves. Nothing was out of the ordinary or unusual about the morning's activities. Around noon we gathered for a delicious homemade lunch of organic ginger-carrot soup, salad, fruit, bread, and a variety of hot teas—a perfect meal to take the edge off the chill of the day.

After a lengthy, leisurely lunch, we reassembled for the afternoon activities. Once back in the room, the facilitator announced, "For the next twenty minutes, we are going to do a meditation. No words will be spoken; there will be only the sound of the beat of a drum. You are to just go 'out there' wherever you choose. The meditation time will end when you hear the fast, repetitive, eight-beat sequence of the drum. At that time, bring yourselves back to this room. You will have five minutes to write or draw anything you experienced. Now please find a comfortable place to lie on the floor."

Being the good, obedient student I am, I found an ideal spot lying diagonally between several others on the wooden floor. I pulled my legs up to my torso to flatten my swayed back. I was grateful we had had plenty of time since lunch because I imagined myself falling fast asleep in this comfortable position.

The beat of the drum was a primal, consistent, pounding rhythm like a heartbeat. In my mind's eye, I found myself wandering around in total blackness and decided to see just how fast I could go. There was absolutely nothing but blackness everywhere I looked. The speed at which I was travelling was faster than any speed I have experienced on any amusement park ride. I felt as if I were sitting atop a rocket headed deep into outer space.

Suddenly, another rocket caught up with me to my left. I was somewhat stunned and frightened when I realized the person atop the other rocket was Micah. The image I saw showed him in a white T-shirt and fedora, his giant brown eyes quickly gazing at me and then looking away. No words transpired between us; he simply nodded in a forward direction, and together the two of us traveled side by side even faster through the blackest of black space. A part of me jolted, realizing I was lying on the floor of the room of the retreat center, while another part of me said, "Relax, let's go!" I completely relaxed, turning down the resistant part of my brain.

We continued traveling at high speed when suddenly, without words, we both slowed down to a complete stop, facing only blackness. Simultaneously, we stepped off the rockets and began walking side by side in the same direction in the darkness; then we stopped. Standing to my left, he reached across me with his left arm, extending his hand to a place in the blackness that opened inward like a door. He gestured with a nod of the head for me to enter ahead of him.

As I stepped in, I could not believe my eyes! The interior space was filled with a blinding brilliance—it was full of radiant light. I felt the presence of my son to my back as he intimated to me that he wanted to show me this healing place. As I scanned the space, I was awestruck by the immense feeling of love, calm, peace, and belonging.

Directly in front of me, I saw a massive, multifaceted diamond-shaped structure that on first impression appeared to be a healing table. Though faceted, the structure was clear, round to ovoid on the top, and conical looking from the side—literally like a colossal diamond. As my eyes continued scanning, I saw at least seven very tall, white, crystalline-like benevolent beings, all with blue eyes of varying shades and shapes. They had heads with ears but no hair, and they had faces with eyes and other features that looked similar to those of a human face—but with only a line for a mouth. They communicated telepathically, and they were standing on the other side and at the ends of the giant diamond healing table, as if they were *waiting* for me.

Immediately, I felt the benevolence of their communication and understood somehow that they had helped Micah heal. His desire was to introduce me to them so I could learn their method of healing and heal also.

About that time, through my mind's eye, these benevolent beings showed me laser-like white rays emitting from my hand. They helped me to know that I could move and remove the dark spots that are the color of capers and the size of garbanzo beans and that appear energetically as nodules carried life to life, dimension to dimension, incarnate or discarnate in the soul signature—the dark spots that are the root cause of illness or emotional dysfunction showing up today.

Both of my hands felt hot and continued to get hotter, as if a razor-sharp, heavy beam were penetrating the center of my palms. I heard "alikening to John of God" as the loud, repetitive, eight-beat sound coming from the drum abruptly took me from my lessons with the benevolent beings and brought me back to the floor I was lying on.

Holy smokes! What just happened? I thought to myself, as I took the next moments of silence to draw and write in my journal. Naturally, I mused over my intense experience, the feelings and images, to understand exactly what had just occurred. I knew of John of God, the Brazilian healer, having watched *Healing: The Movie* in my worldwide studies of indigenous healing. But I had never felt drawn to him. I wrote in my journal: "Add visit to John of God to punch list."

My mind was still focused on the extravagant journey I had taken when the facilitator interrupted with the next exercise. But try as I might, nothing was going to take my mind and feelings away from continuing to process the event I'd had. I had clearly gone somewhere—but where? Why?

When I asked myself these questions, I repeatedly heard that my son wanted me to know that he had met these beings in his "process" on the other side of the veil, and because of his love for me—his knowing how desperately I longed to heal and help others—he simply wanted to show me who had helped him and make me aware of the place where they were.

No matter what the facilitators did the remainder of the day, I stayed in my microcosm until the group was asked to make a big circle again, this time inside because the skies had opened up outside. We held hands and did a closing prayer. Before leaving, the facilitator gave all participants an opportunity to announce any upcoming programs, workshops, events, or messages for the group as we went around the circle.

I happened to be standing between two persons that I had not yet met. The woman to my right released my hand, stepped forward, and announced she would be taking a group of people to see John of God in April 2013!

My whole body weakened, and I could feel myself falling to the floor when the woman to my left pulled up hard on my arm, enabling me to catch myself. I was still reeling from the experience earlier in the day, and I knew it was not by chance that I was now standing next to a total stranger who had just announced an upcoming trip to see John of God—a name I had heard a mere two hours prior. A visit to John of God was now imminent!

For days I could still see the faces of the benevolent crystalline white beings with vibrant blue eyes. I might be driving down the road when suddenly, the face of one would appear on my windshield. To this day, I often see these beings in my dreams or in my mind's eye. I sense the feeling in the air if one or more of them are nearby— there is nothing else like it.

My 12-12-12 experience is imprinted deeply in my being, never to be forgotten!

47

The Best Christmas Ever

Most people who know me know that I like to do a winter solstice ritual on December 21 each year. The shortest day of the year, it's a time of reflection, a time of deep thanks and gratitude, and a time to release all that I choose not to take with me into the next year—so that I may grow personally, spiritually, and in any other facet I need. Sometimes, I do a formal gathering with others, but most often, I do my ritual alone.

I had forewarned my cousin Kay, who was visiting from Texas for Christmas, that I would do my early-morning ceremony alone but that later in the evening, when I did my group gathering, she was free to join me—which she did. Lydia, Rock's daughter, wasn't coming in from Cleveland for Christmas until the twenty-second, so my traditional morning ritual would be uninterrupted by holiday family guests.

On December 21, 2012, at about 5:30 a.m. (EST), the veil was very, very thin. I decided to be outside in the quiet of the dark early morning, where surprisingly, I physically met my son! I could feel him in the air nearby. Then shortly afterward, I heard a voice say, "I am right behind you." Instinctively, I turned my palms backward behind me and touched an energy field of high vibration, which reverberated throughout my body. My physical body was electrified. I knew this energy-being was Micah, and he knew I knew.

I anchored my feet firmly on the earth, grounding myself so I could maintain this vibrational connection longer. I felt his deep, unconditional love for me as our forms melded together. I was astounded at his efforts to ensure that we met and "hugged" in this manner before he moved on to his next soul mission. Everything I had missed about doing or having with him during our physical life, I experienced in an instant—sleepovers, driver's ed, prom, college graduation, birthdays, family vacations, holidays, sharing in his children's lives, normalcy, happiness, joy—all melded together in a kaleidoscope of sight and immense feeling, as if desired past events and hoped-for future events blended into us in this infinitesimal moment in time.

I felt it was time for him to leave, and I could feel our energy bodies release the hug. Tears of joy gently rolled down my cheeks as I thanked Micah and I thanked God for this gift.

Despite all the challenges and hardships of addiction, wholeness and healing do exist—on this side or the other! It is up to each one of us to understand our role in the infirmity, have the desire to change ourselves through free will, open our mind's eye to unfathomable possibilities, work toward healing—and in God's time, experience what can be.

I had the best Christmas ever! And I know going forward that I will be whole and happy through the holidays, no matter where I am or what I'm doing.

48

John of God

Abadiâna, Brazil (April 2013)

In April 2013, along with six others, I made the long journey from Charlotte, North Carolina, to Abadiâna, Brazil, to meet and work with Medium João Teixeira, commonly known in English as John of God. To my shock and amazement, I learned that one of my fellow soul-journers was Jeremy, the father of Curtis, who had passed in February 2012! Was it coincidence? Or had Micah and Curtis collaborated to get the two of us there? At this point, I simply accepted the extremely low odds of the incident as a phenomenon and credited God for its occurrence.

I had no idea what to expect but was overwhelmed to discover that the Casa—the spiritual healing center where John of God does his work—is situated atop a large crystalline formation unlike anything else in the world. Formally named Casa de Dom Ignacio de Loyola, its colors are white and blue. The pictures of Jesus, Mother Mary, various saints and entities associated with the Casa, and John of God all have startling blue eyes.

With no hesitation at all, I found the place that my son had showed me on 12-12-12. Never before had I experienced such holiness, magnitude, and pure love seeping from the ground, dripping from the sky, and manifesting so humbly in Medium João and the loving entities incorporated in John of God.

The weekend before I left the United States, Oprah had aired her visit to John of God, lending credibility to the energy and healing work that occurs on the sacred grounds of the Casa. But for me, no television show or book could possibly replicate the experience of the magic that occurs at the Casa and in Abadiâna. Medium João continually reminds the visitors to the Casa that he does not heal anyone: the one who heals is God, who in His infinite goodness allows the entities to use Medium João as a tool, providing healing and consolation to all brothers and sisters.

Everyone is welcomed no matter what their religious beliefs or cultural convictions. Medium João is an instrument in God's Divine Hands. All beings, incarnate or discarnate, deserve healing and wholeness, and many seem to know that the Casa and the surrounding grounds are a divine place for this to occur. In the words of Christ in John 15:12: "This is my commandment: Love one another as I have loved you." This teaching is palpable at the Casa.

When I first went before John of God, I could not stop crying. The room, the people, John of God himself, and the air surrounding me were so holy and filled with pure, unconditional love that I felt I got a glimpse of what this love could be, as if I were standing before Jesus. Once I composed myself, engaging him eye to eye, he took my right hand, gently rubbing the emerald ring I wear in honor of Micah's life. In that instant, I felt that everything that could possibly be known about me, in this lifetime or any other, was known.

My request was to heal the lineage of addiction that had taken the life of my son and to bring advanced knowledge and awareness of healing addiction to this planet. In the seconds that passed, the translator spoke my request, and while Medium João (who only speaks Portuguese) continued to hold my hand, a voice spoke through his mouth in English, firmly saying, "I wiiillll helllpp you." Then Medium João quickly resumed giving instructions in Portuguese.

I felt awestruck—it was as if I were in a time warp. But I was brought back to reality by Vinicius Turk, my translator, who told me to meet him outside after the morning session and that he would convey the details of John of God's instructions.

I spent two weeks in the marvel and sacredness of this place. The spirits of Micah and my mother, Jewel, were present much of the time I was there. At the Casa, I became aware of the difference between energy healing and spiritual healing. I had the grand *"Aha!"* moment and the sacred teaching that before his death—when I saw large, dark blobs in Micah's energy field—the beings represented by those blobs could not have been removed simply by my shooing them away. The dark beings in his field were "spirit attachments," the least of which caused no more than a diminishment of Micah's energy, and the greatest of which allowed the spirit to gain total control of his life!

Whatever the intensity of the attachment, such a spirit drains a person's mental and physical energy and impairs his or her existence and goals, even to the point of causing the death of that person. The attaching spirit uses the host's life force to remain on the earthly plane, and in so doing, it manipulates the host's body and mind. Each case of spirit attachment is unique, with as many varieties and complexities as there are human lives. While each spirit attachment is unique, the underlying principle remains the same for all of them: a spirit attachment's purpose is usually to satisfy some form of physical desire.

A dependency habit developed over a lifetime—such as a dependency on smoking, drugs, alcohol, food, or obsessive sex—is one of the most common causes of attachment. A craving spirit will attach itself to a host who has a similar dependency in order to satisfy the craving that is still imprinted in the spirit's personality. This is the most difficult type of attachment to dislodge. Depending on the extent of the craving—like that of heroin—the influence exerted on the host can be anything from aggravating to devastating.

The worst examples appear in the spirits of fully dependent drug abusers who must still satisfy their craving *after death*. There are plenty of incarnate drug addicts who are open to the attachment of a drug-dependent spirit, and most of them are *completely unaware* of this spiritual phenomenon. One feeds off the other, and there is no hope of dispelling the attachment unless the host is willing to give up the habit, which is highly unlikely.

In my request to John of God, I was provided with information that I never knew existed when Micah was still alive. When I presented myself and my desire to heal a lineage of addiction, I got exactly what I asked for. Now I had to be awake and aware of anything else I might be called to do. My instructions from John of God included an admonition to maintain a disciplined approach to prayer and meditation and also to have focus and be open to working with the highly evolved entities.

I returned to Charlotte in something of a fog. For over two weeks, I had lived among high-vibrational beings dedicated to the healing and consolation of the great pain and suffering experienced by humans in today's world. I witnessed miracles each day. I saw people get out of wheelchairs and walk out of the building. I saw eye scrapings and hemostats placed up the nose and deep into the head of individuals desiring to receive physical surgeries.

I talked to people who had made multiple journeys to Abadiâna to receive the healing they desired. Numerous stories came from those healed of cancer, including children who were not given long to live by Western medicine but who had returned to keep their little bodies balanced and restored to perfection.

I also experienced my own spiritual surgery, which was nothing less than miraculous. The fact that I'd asked for one thing—the healing of my lineage—didn't mean that one thing was all I was going to get. The entities take care of what they see, usually prioritizing the soul's healing over the physical; I was told that I needed surgery to prevent a problem that I would have in the future that would keep me from my soul's mission. Even though my mind knew I had received no physical cuts, scrapes, or probes, it still had to adjust to the physical pain my body experienced from the "invisible" surgery on my spine.

Returning to my routine physical existence in Charlotte was difficult at first; it took about three weeks for me to integrate. Those around me seemed deeply asleep and unaware of anything except their cell phones, text messages, and Facebook comments. Although I felt saddened about not having known about spirit healing before, I continually prayed for answers and asked if there were anything else I could do to help Micah's soul.

Over the next weeks and months, I was taught that one must work with the host and the spirit attachment(s) for true healing to occur. In all my years of learning, I had never come across anything like this. But innately, I knew that the highest good of all was for *all*—not just some—to be restored to Divine health. It didn't matter if they were perceived to be light or dark, good or evil—all deserved healing.

49

The Agreement

(September 2013)

One night as I lay in bed, daydreaming before drifting off to sleep, I was startled to feel an all-too-familiar energy that I had believed I was long done with. The feeling was electrical; my mind and eyes worked, but the energy was causing the rest of my physical body to freeze. I knew I needed to get a strong grip on my energy field to keep this outside interference at bay. Why in God's name was this presence showing up in my life again?

I associated the presence of this energy with a very difficult time in my life, a time when I learned many lessons about the invisible world the hard way. Back then I naively opened myself up to anything I thought could or would help me learn healing—specifically healing that would help my son. But the beings that showed up took far too great a degree of control of my energy body for their own purposes, acting in a very careless, manipulative manner and discounting and ignoring the impact on my physicality.

At the time, I became appalled at the invasiveness of their nature, and despite their threatening antics, I succeeded in removing them from my life. Now, eight years later, they were tapping on my door again.

I had grown and developed by leaps and bounds in my understanding of the workings of the spiritual world, and I stood strongly in my own power. Later in the week after this incident, I asked the help of more evolved and powerful beings—specifically archangels—to assist me in removing this energy from my being once and for all. In response, I "heard" that I had an agreement with these careless beings—and they wanted me to fulfill it. Yeah, right! Fat chance! I was not about to open up that can of worms again.

I called upon divine help from everywhere I could think of. I stated out loud that I was consciously unaware of *any* agreement, and as of this moment, I declared any such claim to be *null and void*. I had no *intention* to fulfill *anything* with this energy form.

Admittedly, I felt pretty good about myself and went about my life with no concerns about these beings lingering at the edge of my energy field. Days and weeks passed with no thoughts about or energetic sensitivities to them. However, something in the back of my mind queried whether or not Micah was a part of this.

One day in early November, while sitting at my desk, I was gently nudged to research Spirit Releasement Therapy. I was interested to learn more about it—and I should have known that in being so strongly guided to do this, there would be yet another unknown gift lurking in the wings.

After three days of reading, researching, reviewing books online, and reading practitioner websites word for word, I was attracted to a specific practitioner who appeared highly skilled and qualified. Once we connected, I felt this woman was a soul sister, someone I had known a long time and someone I knew I was divinely guided to work with. We scheduled an appointment for later that week.

During our session, I felt somewhat nervous and anxious, but I was curious to see how she did what she did and what would show up. Although I was stepping into unknown territory, I felt comfortably guided.

Much to my amazement, my son was present for this gathering. Surprisingly, he did not feel vibrant and vivacious as he had previously. I also observed another human being in discarnate form, unknown to me, constantly at Micah's side, as if attached. I did not know it at the time, but the work to be done with this practitioner was more in-depth lineage healing.

Surprisingly, the negative energy beings were present also. I was stunned to learn that one of them had been "assigned" to Micah and was most likely the big dark blob that I had seen so frequently when Micah was alive and strung out on heroin.

I continued to follow the practitioner's lead. I realized in my own consciousness that I could see darkness in light and light in darkness. My heart opened wide, expressing deep compassion for the dark beings who believed they were just doing what they were supposed to be doing. My physical body opened to such an immense level of emotional compassion that I began crying, sobbing for the group of dark beings that had presented themselves for healing and restoration to wholeness.

The softness and gentleness with which they participated was nothing like what I had expected or witnessed in my earlier encounters with them. The being that was attached to Micah gracefully and willingly released itself from Micah and drifted off with the others. The presence of Archangel Michael, Jesus, and Mother Mary shined brightly as I realized the other human being at Micah's side was one he had attached to in order to fulfill his continued craving for heroin. It was as though Micah could go no further on the other side if this healing did not occur.

This revelation was almost more than I could comprehend. Micah seemed to be fighting against all odds to get my attention to fulfill an agreement—still unknown to me—that would break the cycle of addiction in our lineage and also heal a group of beings whose time it was to be complete—restored to wholeness. Without the teachings I had received and the willingness of the more highly evolved entities of John of God to help me, I do not see how any of this would ever have happened.

In the days that followed, I could not help reflecting on Dr. Taylor's report from the early nineties, when Micah was so young: *"In describing his drawing, Matt suggested a story of an individual with a great deal of self-denial wanting to HELP and HEAL other persons and expressing few fears or inadequacies, and a great deal of self-denial."*

Micah's message is powerful for those who choose to embrace the invisible and who are willing to do the work to heal the invisible epidemic of heroin addiction in today's society. As mind-blowing and impossible as all of this seems, the Hero did return with information to heal and help others—in a style unique to my beloved Micah Aaron Matthew Felcman.

May God remember the soul of my son,
who has gone to his eternal home.
In loving testimony to his life,
I pledge charity to help
perpetuate ideals important to him.

Through such deeds, and through prayer and memory,
is his soul bound up in the bond of life.
I am grateful for the sweetness of his life and for what
he did accomplish.

May Micah Aaron Matthew Felcman rest in dignity and peace.
Amen[1]

---

[1] From a Jewish prayer known as a *Yizkor*, which means "in memory of the dearly departed ones." This version is from Menorah Chapels in Staten Island, New York.

PART THREE

The Hero's Innermost Cave: Writings of Micah Aaron Matthew Felcman

Untitled

(Age 11)

Shine on me, sunshine.
Rain on me, rain.
Fall softly, dewdrops
and cool my brow again.

Storm, blow me from here
with your fiercest wind.
Let me float across the sky
until I rest again.

Fall gently, snowflakes
cover me with white,
cold icy kisses and
let me rest tonight.

Sun, rain, curving sky
mountain, oceans, leaf, and stone
star shine, moon glow
You're all that I call my own.

Stay or Go

(Age 12)

We all have the choice to stay
or go, but what is up ahead
one will never know.

You can live a life of happiness
and fun or you can live a life
of danger and guns.

Whether you live easy or have
to break boulders, remember the
choice is only on your shoulders.

Hugs

(Age 13)

It's wondrous what a hug can do.
A hug can cheer you when you're blue.
A hug can say, "I love you so."
or, "Gee, I hate to see you go."

A hug is, "Welcome back again!"
and "Great to see you!" or
"Where've you been?"
A hug can soothe a small child's pain
and bring a rainbow after rain.

There's no doubt about it,
we scarcely could survive without it.
A hug delights and warms and charms.
It must be why God gave us arms.

Kittens crave them. Puppies love them.
Heads of State are not above them.
A hug can break the language barrier
and make the dullest day seem merrier.

Costumed Couples

When I was growing up,
my parents,
for the most part,
managed to drink
daily.

Beer mostly,
sometimes
wine
and liquor
on occasion.

A lot of the time,
they would have
fancy little dinner
parties,
dress up in
costumes,
sometimes with themes,
and everyone came
in couples.

Sometimes
the couples
would bring
their children.

Most of the time
they left them
at home
with babysitters or maids.

Leaving myself
to be found
wandering
aimlessly
amongst the drunkards.

Watching them spill.
Listening to them slur.
Completely curious.
Another weekend,
another party,
another theme,

with the focus
on
margaritas.

Milk jugs
full of
frozen margaritas
neatly
stashed in the cooler
underneath
the bar.

This time,
this weekend,
this party,
this theme,
my parents stuck me
in
a costume.

I was the bartender.

When the
costumed couples
needed a refill,
they came to the bar.

I would reach
into the cooler,
grab a jug,
then replenish
their booze.

I even had
a tip jar.
They thought of everything.

Somewhere,
in between pouring,
counting tips,
and feeling like a part
of the theme,
I decided to
hit one of the jugs.

I remember
it tasting like
a
lime frosty
with a bite.

Like the bite you get
from cough medicine.

I don't know
how many times

I hit the jug,
but I sure as hell
remember the feeling.

The room
was a spinning
roller coaster,
infested with
couples in costumes,

and the theme,

margaritas.

A Brief Introduction

I was brought
into this world
on
May 17th, 1979
at 5:10 a.m. CST
in the small
West Texas town
of
Lubbock.

My mother's firstborn
and
my father's second son,
I was welcomed
into a broken home.

Just days
after arriving,
my folks decided to relocate
back to Houston,
and
still, to this day,
I have never returned
to the place of my birth.

So for the most part,
I have always
considered myself
to be a Houstonian.

Plus
both
of
my parents
were born in Houston,
and
many of my grandparents
were born
in the Lone Star state as well.

To make a long story short,
I'm either
a 9th- or 10th-
generation Texan.

Anyway,
our family
wasn't in Houston
for all that long
before my dad's company
transferred us to Singapore.

I started school
in Southeast Asia
and
lived there until
the age of five,
maybe four.

Thanks to my father's job,
our family
was relocated
on quite
the regular basis.

I was never
in the same school
for
more than a year growing up,
so
I was always the new kid on the block.

Believe me,
constantly being
the new kid
had all kinds
of
ups and downs.

The worst part
was
forming friendships
or
having a girlfriend,
and
knowing that any day now,
I would be moving
halfway across the globe.

On the other hand,
it taught me
the skills of communication.
I was never shy
and
never had trouble
when it came to meeting people
and
fitting in.

By the time I was fourteen,
I had lived in
Texas, Singapore, Colorado,
the Middle East,
Louisiana, Los Angeles,
Virginia, North Carolina,
and
I had spent
a lot of time
in
Israel,
South Africa,
France,
Germany, India,
Cyprus,
and forty-four
of
the fifty states.

Anyway,
for the most part,
I was always a good kid
growing up,
and
never really causing
any trouble.
I always made good grades
and
always participated
in all different types
of
athletics.

However,
it seems that everything changed
in our family
when we moved
to Charlotte, North Carolina,
from Los Angeles, California.

It was at this stage
of the game when my parents
had decided
to get a divorce,
and
I was just entering
the dark world
of drug addiction.

I was about fourteen years old,
and
this is when
my life
turned into a series
of
war stories.

Outcast

Life seemed on the up-and-up, and all was going well until my father came home one day to tell us we were moving from LA to Charlotte, North Carolina. I can't speak for my mother, but I was fucking crushed.

It was the early nineties, and I was around fourteen years old and perfectly happy spending the rest of my life in Southern California. I had just made the football team at my new private school in Anaheim, had landed the girlfriend I wanted, was establishing my popularity, and already had the reputation for being the crazy poet who held nothing back when given a pen and blank piece of paper. All of this came crashing down. Within one week, all of these things faded into memories, and I was on a plane landing in Charlotte.

Once again I was the new kid, starting a new school, had no friends, and very quickly felt lost in the concrete-lacking, Bible Belt town of South Charlotte, America. What was hip and cool in LA was not hip and cool on the East Coast. I was almost instantly labeled an outcast and weirdo. I had gone from being a popular, football-playing poet to a "nobody," and I didn't know how to deal with it.

It was at this point in my life when I came up with the chameleon coping mechanism. If you told me something was cool, I would blend right into it with the goal of becoming cool for you. If you have never tried this coping mechanism—don't! It steals your soul because the more you change to please others, the more you lose track of your true self. I honestly believe that this coping technique is what caused me to try drugs in the first place. God, if I could only go back in time and use my balls to stand up for **what I thought was cool . . . what I thought was hip.**

Back in those days, education was a priority, sports was a priority, and betting my allowance on baseball games with my father was a priority. All of that disappeared so fast, it baffles me. It almost seems like overnight, all of that changed, and this new image, this shell of character, had taken over my soul, taken over my passion—and I wasn't so blinded by the thought of being cool that I couldn't realize that my entire life was crumbling underneath me.

So at my new private school in Charlotte, I had slipped to the ranks of outcast. The only friends I made were also outcasts and were as far as possible from the sporty, popular kids we referred to as the Glory Boys.

This gave me a chance to focus on my writing because my outcast posse consisted of long-haired musicians—what the Glory Boys referred to as Art Fags.

The First Buzz

I told my mother that I was going to the movies with a friend,
and needed about 10 bucks
so I could pay for the movie
and some popcorn.
When my mom dropped me off at the theatre,
my buddy was sitting outside, waiting for my arrival.
As my mother drove off,
my friend asked me if I wanted to just skip the movie
and split a bag of herb.
I had never smoked weed in my life
and really didn't know what the hell he was talking about.
I didn't want him to think that I was some kind of loser,
so I said, "Sure, to hell with the movie."
Next thing I know, Doug (my friend—yeah, right)
stole some rolling papers from the drugstore,
and we proceeded to wander off into the woods
behind the movie theatre.
So here I am, sitting in the woods,
watching Doug roll what would be the first joint
to ever cross my path.
I remember it being dark,
so I really didn't get a good look
at what was in the plastic baggy.
By this time, I knew that we were about to smoke pot,
and I started to get a little nervous.
All these thoughts and tales of drugs
that I had been told in school and by my parents
began racing through my head.
Now the joint was burning,
and I remember watching Doug smoke it,

but not how you smoke a cigarette.
He was taking enormous puffs,
holding them in as long as he could and coughing furiously.
After he hit it a few times, he passed the joint my way,
and butterflies rocked my stomach.
I smoked cigarettes, so I knew how to inhale smoke,
but the first time I hit the joint, I exhaled too fast.
Doug was quick to tell me that I needed to "hold it in."
So, I did.

Well,
we finished blazing the joint
and walked out of the woods,
back to the theatre.
We had been sitting down
when we were smoking,
and I really didn't feel any kind of high whatsoever.
However,
when I got up and started walking, it all hit me at once.
I felt like I was walking beside myself,
like I was floating.
Then I just started laughing for no reason.
Everything seemed hilarious,
and I realized that I loved everything about being high.
My mother picked me up from the theatre
and had no idea that
I was higher than a kite.
I think I laughed all the way home,
and when I got home,
I ate a whole bag of potato chips dipped in ketchup.
I remember sleeping like a baby that night,
and when I woke up, I called Doug to check and see
if there was any weed left over.

Since I paid for half of the bag,
I wanted my half.
I went by his house,
and he put my half in a separate bag,
and just like that,
I was hooked.

Evil Seeds

The
ever so perilous,
painstaking
realms
of addiction,
how they capture
thy soul,
love, and mind.
How they
discriminate
to no one,
poor,
beautiful,
rich, or deformed.
Suffered by
none other than
the scum,
I think not.
Seen destroying
the power elite,
see,
she
has
no boundaries.

Endless life,
married,
surrounded daily
by sorrow,
sadness,
loneliness,

and self.
Happiness hidden,
if at all
it exists,
too many symptoms,
like books lined
on the shelves.

Destroyer through history,
traced to the beginning
of time,
destroyer
of
lifestyles,
family, income,
appetite, confidence,
consumer of passion
and soul.

I only
speak
of these battles,
for I confess,
I have been there before.
Lost from
lovers, mother, father,
and
goals,
yet continued.
Insanity defined,
madness,
expecting different results,
justifying
my

rapid descent.
Think not
almighty strength within,
rationalize failure
thee demons
inside again,
for we are addicted.

Whether it is
sex, drugs,
booze,
or
food,
gambling,
stealing,
sir, 'tis thee
who owns this soul.
A prisoner.

World
of experience,
growing,
expanding,
brought to an end.
15 years of age,
this begins,
15 years of age
is where I stand,
for there
shall be
no
expansion.

Alongside these
addictions,
weaknesses,
introductions have been made,
greeted by
handcuffs,
jail cells,
depression,
accompanied by rage.
See
this is
the reality
ignored.

From the Asians
with their
opiates,
South Americans
and
their coke,
the Roman Empire
consuming their
wines,
Native Americans
and
their
smoke,
for I
have been
all of these.
This
is nothing more
than a disease,

no known cure
as soon
as
you
plant
the Devil's seed,
the weed
that never dies.
We welcome
you to struggles, hate,
never-ending pain,
never plant the seed again,
for it longs
to control thee.

For we all
are born
with
gorgeous, golden spoons
in our mouths.
When this
evil seed
is planted,
quickly
it
shall be taken out.
The lucky ones
are soon to be
replaced
with
silver,
however, for many,
the seed accepts this
not either.

With another chance
comes the plastic spork,
the overpowering
seed shall break
the ends,
eliminating your fork.
Suddenly
stranded alone
with
a
plastic spoon,
no longer
roof overhead,
the world
becomes your room,
for
the seed
keeps
this promise.

Let Us Dance

(This is what Micah left to do when he left the
intensive care unit and went to Atlanta.)

Night clubs

over flowing

XTC,
and ravers
wearing their wide
leg
pants,
dancing,
mopping

the floors.

Some with glow sticks,

some of them adults chewing on pacifiers.

Blame it on the lights,
drugs,

better yet,
blame it on fucked-up childhoods.

Everything has a reason!

"I love you, Brother."

"Nope, you don't even know me. Just listen to the music because that is why we are here."

DJ's, turntables, sound, creation,

the drugs are for expanding
of
one's imagination . . .

So, let us dance.

Consequences

Youth has ended, and all the charm
has withered away with the cocktails, cigarettes,
pills, drugs,
but most of all the asphalt.
It's become painful.
Well beyond depressing and I really
can't understand how I roll out of bed
day after day.
All the jail cells,
Heroin overdoses,
Cocaine overdoses,
Liver failures,
Methadone clinics,
Hookers,
Guns,
Bad poems,
Relationships,
Shared fluids,
Shared needles,
Fights,
and
Failures.
How am I still alive?
I've tasted gun oil!
I've put a loaded gun to my head
15 years ago and didn't have the balls
to pull the trigger.
I don't have the balls today
either.
All of the bridges heroin burned,
all the lost

broken souls.
Josh had the balls to smash
a .38 against his sweaty temple
and let one fly.
God, Bless Him!
Van Gogh had the balls;
Hemingway, Kurt Cobain
had the balls.
DAMN!
All it takes is a fraction of a second
and this whole,
mad day-to-day living
is over.
HELL,
I don't even have enough cash
to buy a .38
in order to put one through my
never-ending headache, right now.
I don't want the balls of Van Gogh,
Hemingway, Cobain, and Josh.
I want the words of Blake, Wordsworth,
Yeats, Saul, Williams, Sage Francis,
Whitman, Keats, Maya Angelou, Bukowski;
all crammed into my tiny writing ability.
Erato, find my blue Bic and pages.
I wanna study every style of writing
to put off the .38 for one
more painful day.
Erato...
My Dear Erato,
I lost all connection with you
and I swear to all the Gods
that our separation brings that
damn .38 closer,

and closer.
It's that connection,
relationship,
that saves my soul on an
hourly basis.
Hell, Van Gogh had heart
and balls!
It takes some serious heart
to cut off your ear.
Hell, to cut off anything!
The grain stacks got to him!
The canvas no longer called out
his name, and his Muse left
along with his ear and brain matter.
Just like that! His heart was
broken and the consequences of
creativity raped his passion.
The poor bastard!
Why didn't he cut off his hands?
Why didn't he just cut out
his heart and stab it with one of
his funny horsetail bristled paint brushes?
Why couldn't Hemingway leave the shotgun
at home and just fish for one more day?
His Muse accepted his homosexuality
but he wouldn't.
He put the hook in his mouth and died like
a fish out of water with the Gods and Muses both
at his side!
And, all they could say was,
"Another victim of the consequence
of creativity."
How could I forget about
the true GONZO journalist?

Hunter S. found the balls
to bounce one through his
fear and loathing mentality.
The difference here
is Hunter took his Muse
with him. And so did Bukowski.
Bukowski died a natural death
far from a .38.
He and Hunter were the last of their
kind and they took their Muses
to the grave with 'em.
You hear that, Erato?

They took their Muses to the soil
along with their pens, pages,
and creativity.
I'll latch onto your soul, Erato,
like a leech, as we fear and loathe
through these pages, until they put
us into the soil together, too.
I have two beautiful kids, Erato
and I need to be there for them
one of these days when I get
my shit together.
Cobain left his poor daughter
to grow up alone without the wisdom
and talent of her father.
All she knows is Dad couldn't
take it anymore—the heroin, depression,
withdrawal, responsibility; but, most of
all the consequence of creativity grabbed
Kurt by the ankles and yanked him
into the soil abyss.
His Muse had long moved on;

On to a much more promising
soul . . .
one with less balls but
more heart and dedication.
A soul, reborn and ready to face
the drowning reality of creativity,
without an ounce of fear to
be detected.
A soul overflowing with expression
and a desire to be heard both
locally and around the world.
A soul, like mine, fighting
sometimes hourly to keep the
.38 at bay. Hell, sometimes fighting
by the minute to keep that
hothead from slicing my
cranium like a hot knife
through butter.
That damn soil abyss is calling
my name, "Dear . . ."
It's screaming
my name because it feels my
weakness and despair.
And every word scribbled across
these pages keeps me from throwing
in the towel and joining the
others.
Erato, you keep me safe.
With you by my side the
world is mine, the journals are
full, and all the blue Bic pens
fear and hide from correction.

I'm Sorry, Daughter

(2006)

You are nine months old
and
barely even know me.
But you need to know that
I'm sorry for being
a drug addict,
an alcoholic,
a car thief,
and a liar.

A cheater,
thief,
writer,
career student,
and
careerless.

I'm sorry for
bringing you
into a world of hate,
terrorism,
crime,
television,
and false reality.

I'm sorry
for being
the man I was
before you entered
this hell,

this search for perfection.

I'm sorry
for the way
I treated your Mother.

I'm sorry if you follow
in my footsteps
instead of your Mother's,
and
I'm sorry that I will
not be able
to protect you
from every single
situation.

I'm sorry that I
even had to write
this
and
sorry if you ever have to
read this.

But understand
that I will never
be sorry for loving,
or
for helping you see
this world through
your eyes.

May you always
lean upon me.

My Children

(Written after Parker was born in 2007)

I found reality
in the soul of a child.
A child
who radiated love and
captured my heart.

I found truth
and
purpose in the
eyes of
an infant.

If anything makes
sense in this God forsaken
world . . .

It is my love for my
children.

Because of You

I'm a selfish writer.
I always talk about myself, my problems,
my ideas, and so forth.

So, I'd like to dedicate these next
several pages to my father,
May he rest in peace.
And to be honest, I don't think
I've ever written or mentioned him in any of my work.
Michael Wayne Felcman,
this is for you.

You were a man's man
and "one hell of a man,"
according to your friends.
I know this because they
told me at your funeral.

You were a tough man,
you fought, you played rugby,
broke bones, and never
flinched or lost
your stride.

You taught me how to be limber
on my feet and quick with my hands.

You would throw a baseball
or football at me as hard as
you could, and would say,
"If you catch a bullet from me,

nobody your age will get a ball
past you."

You said, "If you can touch it,
you can catch it."
and I still believe in these
statements today.

You also taught me that I
had five fouls in basketball
and that I should use them.

You taught me that there are
no rules to a fight, and if someone
starts it, you finish it.

You taught me manners and
to treat women with respect.
Because of you, I open a door
for a lady or pull out her chair
before she sits.

Because of you, I've never
hit a woman and vow
to never even lay so much
as a finger on a woman.

Because of you, I'm dying to read
Catcher in the Rye because I know
it was one of your favorite books.

Because of you, I've learned lessons
that you never did.
I've learned that it's important to

share emotions versus stuffing them,
and I've learned that life is too short
to not speak what's on your mind.

Another lesson that you have taught me
is that you should always tell your
children that you love them because you
never know if you'll see them tomorrow.

Because of your actions, you've taught me
to treat women with respect, and communicate with them,
and tell them if you no longer love them.

You also taught me to make amends
with people as soon as you can
because you may never have the chance
to see them again.

I wish I would have spent more
time with you, Dad.
I wish I would have told you
I loved you.
I wish we could've been friends,
and I wish I could have listened
to all the stories of your life journey.

I wish I would have known
you as a friend and a father
at the same time.
Either way,
I LOVE YOU,
and ALWAYS WILL.

I know you're in a better place now!

Fear and Loathing in Oahu

(June 3, 2009)

Every single night in Waikiki is Saturday night. I moved to this city 100% sober and within one week had access to OxyContin, Xanax, marijuana, salvia, LSD, cocaine, crack, and of course heroin. Within a week of being here, I was eating handfuls of painkillers with a six-pack of beer, a $10 pack of cigarettes, and a $20 bag of kind bud weed, which is something I have not smoked in several years!

Less than a week later, I was shooting 260 milligrams of OxyContin, eating Xanax with beer, and polishing off the night with anywhere from a half to a full gram of shitty island cocaine. (And, when I say polish off, I mean two to four shots straight into the veins.)

I came here with thousands of dollars in my pocket, and now I'm broker than two jokes with no laugh. I am locked in a fucking psych ward getting pumped full of Ativan and 10 mg Valium. I spent more than a month wandering around downtown Honolulu looking for a place to live and some sort of job to line my pockets so I could take care of my bills. I was able to put a roof over my head, but I spent the rest of the time playing middleman, trying to hook people up with drugs to have a few dollars.

It worked for a while, but my heroin addiction took over, and I found myself pounding the pavement with hopes of making enough money to keep from being dope sick. While it worked, I would make enough cash to grab a $15-to-$20 shot of heroin and still have enough cash to grab a pack of cigarettes and three items off the dollar menu at McDonald's.

But, as usual, I ended up dope sick, starving, and smoking other people's butts out of ashtrays all over town. And the sad thing is that it wasn't fun. I had a better time when I first moved to Hawaii and was sober, loaded with cash, and overwhelmed with opportunity.

The sad thing about this addict is no matter how hard I try, drugs manage to find me—plus I am a chronic relapser. I can stay sober for

233

a year and a half, free from all drugs and alcohol, and at some point, that little voice in the back of my head takes control and convinces me that a shot of heroin or an ice-cold beer will make everything fall into place and make life joyful all over again.

When I have been sober for long periods of time, I always justify drinking a beer or a Jameson and Coke with lime, long before I justify a shot of dope or an ear ringer of cocaine.

I came to Oahu with the number-one goal of remaining sober while starting a new life and with high hopes of becoming 100 percent self-sufficient. Now, "self-sufficient" means equipped with the ability to maintain and hold down a job, be a good employee, and take care of myself free from outside financial sources. But even more so, free from the codependency of a woman.

All of my life, I have been supported financially and romantically. How can I ever learn to take care of and love someone else if I can't take care of or love myself?

This junkie is so used to tracking down the closest high and most easily taken-advantage-of women that I don't even have to look anymore. Both of these downfalls manage to find me like some sort of supermagnet, even if my back is turned and my eyes are closed. I don't mean to say that women are downfalls, just the ones that find me and take me under their wing and fall for and listen to all my bullshit.

But I didn't come here to fear and loathe through Oahu. I came here to find salvation within myself. All I want is to be self-sufficient, drug-free, hardworking, honest, talented, focused, healthy, and overwhelmed with good karma—far from self-centered and far from fear and loathing in Oahu.

Here We Go Again

(June 3, 2009)

At this stage of the game, who cares if I live or die? I'm all I have left in this world, and none of that seems to matter, either. In and out of detox facilities, extensive records with behavioral health centers, medical doctors, prescriptions that don't do a damn thing for me. All I know is that these doctors knocked me out.

I came into the ER detoxing from opiates, and they loaded me down with even more opiates and an IV boost of Ativan. Twelve hours later, I found myself waking up in a wheelchair being pushed into a psych hospital with locked doors, tons of crazy people, caffeine-free coffee, and a population of morons doing the Thorazine shuffle. Something has seriously gone wrong with this life!

My biggest dilemma is figuring out how to call work so I can let them know I'm in the loony bin and won't be able to cover my shift at 6:00 p.m. tomorrow. With the luck I'm having, I am going to lose my job altogether, won't be able to pay rent, and will end up homeless in Oahu.

The crazy part about all of this is when they wheeled me into the psych ward, I ran into someone that I knew from the streets. This someone was a girl that I had been on a few dates with before. She is a cute girl, really cool personality. To top it off, she is bipolar and might even be schizophrenic. Whatever! As long as she takes her meds, we can be a couple of crazies roaming through paradise. The only bummer about all of this is that she is checking out today. Damn, she already checked out! What a bunch of shit—she didn't even say good-bye.

Oh well, it is nothing worth throwing the towel in for. To top things off, I just met my nurse . . . my new nurse. The whole shift-change thing throws a kink in my whole system. But I can dig it.

Here's the lowdown. They are giving me Valium, Ativan, vitamins, the nicotine patch, and Nicorette gum. I wonder if I could get away with cheeking my Valium and Ativan? If so, this place is gonna be a lot more fun than I had anticipated. If I cheek them a few days in a row, I can stack up 100+ milligrams and slam them down with a cup of coffee. Now that's a low-grade speedball, if you ask me!

Anyway, back to the madness at hand!

I've been relapsing on opiates since I set foot on this island, and I'm already in a *locked* "mental" ward after only being in Hawaii for a month. The craziest part of it all is that I want to be here. I decided I needed to be checked into this looney-toon, steel-door, pharmie-infested facility in the first place.

I wanted to get off of opiates without putting a bullet through my head. Believe me when I say I was close to tracking down that damn .38 revolver. I've put that fucker off for a few more days thanks to Erato and some other guardian angel that I'm sure I will never meet.

This roller coaster never stops, and we can never get off. So here we go again. Here we go again until someone grabs the courage to unhook their belt and jump off this godforsaken roller coaster.

It's Been Years Since My Last Confession
(June 3, 2009)

Catholicism is probably run by none other than the devil himself, but I'd rather call myself a Catholic than Baptist, Methodist, Lutheran— or Jesus freak, for that matter.

Maybe it is a connection from a prior life that draws me toward the Catholic doctrine and the desire to confess to a father, a priest, on average once a year. Maybe it's because every time I hear about a demonic possession, a Catholic priest is called in to expel the evil souls and send them back to the depths of hell instead of some Bible-thumping, snake-handling Baptist.

Maybe it's because the Catholic Church owns more land worldwide than any other organization and they don't have to pay taxes on them. Plus, they are the largest moneymaker in the world besides the United States government.

To be quite honest, I have no idea why I lean toward Catholicism when it boils down to organized religion. I have studied a lot of Eastern philosophy, read the Koran twice, but still lean toward the faith that revolves around guilt. I don't know the first thing about the afterlife, but I do know when this game is all said and done with, I'm looking to have some sort of spiritual roots attached to my flip-flops before I call it quits.

Who knows? The last confession I completed, the priest jumped down my throat and told me, "You have committed several mortal sins." Which basically means my soul is gonna just burst into flames while the Catholic Church turns its back on me altogether. I don't believe it. I've heard of people being reaccepted back into the Catholic Church after divorce, sins, etc., so maybe I can find a father that will remove my mortal sins and, with the help of God, be guided back through the pearly gates with no questions asked. I need a father who's going to tell me to say a couple Our Fathers with a few Hail Marys and help shove my soul through these mortal sins and back into the acceptance of the almighty and heavenly Catholic Church.

I want to pray the rosary, the whole thing, go to Mass and donate money into those stingy golden saucers that make more money than most working people do in a year. I want to walk up to the altar and have the priest shove the blood and body of Christ into my mouth and say, "Son, you are forgiven. We welcome you to our mass, and may the Lord be with you." "AND ALSO WITH YOU!" I'll shout.

I want to give shit up for the season of Lent just to show the Lord and myself that I'm serious and that I have the heart to deal with sacrifice for the sake of self-growth. I want to become a regular at Mass and confession, and I want to be known as a student of Catholicism, a student whose heart is solid and ready for spiritual expansion.

I want to find myself buried in church activities so I can do whatever it takes to get out of my own sick head/neighborhood. I want to learn how to be honest, free from even white lies, and I want to pay the utmost attention to any and every Bible lesson ever taught. I want the father to feed off of my sincerity and take the time to teach and guide me like an old Kung Fu master; take the time to teach me the tricks and trades of all the old messages.

I'm not saying that I'm going to trade my life for Catholicism; I am saying I am going to rediscover the whole philosophy by jumping in headfirst. At this point of the game, I'm willing, ready, and patient to be open-minded and establish as many spiritual friends and idols as possible.

I truly need help from a power much greater than myself.

Precious Medical Moments

(June 2009)

I just spoke to the doctor here at the mental institution, who recommends that I stick around for at least another one or two days. And I quote, "I know you are not suicidal. You are just a drug addict; you need to be in some sort of treatment center. However, since you have been here, we have loaded up your system with benzos and methadone, and it is our responsibility to send you out of here free from major withdrawal symptoms."

For a moment, I was excited. Nobody in their right mind has any desire whatsoever to rot behind the steel bars of a mental institution when they could be out in the free world smoking cigarettes, eating junk food, and picking up women.

But then it hit me. I don't have enough cash to buy McDonald's, much less a pack of smokes, or the ability to take a chick out for a date. Hell, I'm probably better off sticking around the loony bin for another 30 years. At least I'll end up with three hots and a cot every single day.

And, if I'm lucky, I can keep a good benzo habit on a steady pace, compliments of the nursing staff.

Today, they told me they were lowering my benzo dose and were just going to stick me with two to three Valium per day, chased with Ambien at night. Now it's 7:30 p.m., and I'm counting down the hours until they place those beautiful little pills into my palm and watch me swallow them down like a piece of turkey smothered in homemade cranberry sauce! When I wake up, I have the ability to tell these jokers that I'm done and that I'm straight-up ready to sign myself outta here!

The really hard part lies in the fact that I'm not ready to sign myself out! I need to stay in this place as long as possible while focusing on some sort of massive recovery plan. I guess I'll figure all of this shit out tomorrow! I feel all alone in this world! But the real crazy part is that I feel more comfortable in this crazy house than I do at my own home.

I kept bugging my nurse to give me just two minutes with the doctor, and believe it or not, I finally got those precious moments to speak my mind with Captain Medicine. This damn doctor was going to let me leave today, hungover on benzos and Ambien with no plan lined up whatsoever. I've only been in this place for a couple of days, and there is no way in hell all of the opiates and drugs are out of my system.

I honestly begged the doctor to keep me here for at least another four days—and the crazy bastard agreed. I told the doctor that I want all of the benzos out of my system before they open the doors and let me out of here. The guy actually agreed with me and told me that by Monday, there should be no drugs in my system and that I'll be free to leave.

However, since I am voluntarily admitted, I can check myself out at any point: just sign the paperwork, turn in my crazy-person scrubs, and stroll outta here like nothing ever happened.

Damn, I wish I could stay in this place forever. Set up shop and be the local resident at the nuthouse, teaching all the new crazies the rules, guidelines, and obligations! I could be king of the crazy house, old-timer of the loony bin.

I would know all of the tricks of the trade and would run this place like the joint. I would be trading desserts for medications and trading medications for trays and other meds like Xanax, Ambien, Valium, Ativan, muscle relaxers, and whatever else could line my pockets and keep me king of the loony bin.

June 22, 2009

(Around 5:30 a.m.)

This very moment, I find myself sitting on the concrete steps outside of my tiny house in Honolulu, Hawaii, writing these lines while a cigarette rests between the fingers of my left hand.

Now when I say "my tiny house," I mean where I live—not that it's a house I own. I merely pay rent along with three others—$600, all bills included. The tiny house we live in is at the very end of Waikiki and is seriously one of the only houses in Waikiki. See, Waikiki is a part of Honolulu like Brooklyn is a part of NYC. And Waikiki is also one of the most expensive places to live, similar to San Fran, Boston, or Manhattan, which is why I share a tiny house with three other people. This house only has one bedroom that has two sets of bunk beds, a 10- by 8-foot living room, 12- by 4-foot kitchen, and a bathroom about the size of a public handicapped bathroom.

The people I share this house with just so happen to be an all-right group of guys. Each one of them has led a wild life that if written in book format, I would be more than willing to read. However, before I get into my roommates and Waikiki and the rest of the pages to follow, I would like to explain how I ended up in Waikiki to begin with.

Around this exact date about two months ago, I was sitting in the driver's seat of my Nissan Murano in quite a serious predicament. See, my wife had locked me outta the house and had no intention of ever letting me back into the house—or her life, for that matter. To be honest, I can't say that I blame her, either. This time two months ago, I was in full-blown heroin addiction and was smoking crack, shooting crack, and eating pharmaceuticals like they were the last pills on earth.

I would like to take a time-out here to explain that in a matter of days, I had shot an entire bottle of vinegar because you need something acidic to break the crack down into a shootable solution.

So, here I am sitting in my vehicle, locked out from my wife, the roof I had over my head, and hell, even from my cat. But the really disgusting thing is that all I could think about was that next high. That next hit of crack or shot of heroin to keep my addiction satisfied. You need to understand that I'm sitting in my car with nothing but my clothes, a pillow and blanket, a journal, and a painting I inherited from my father. Oh, I had my Mac computer in the car as well—a MacBook Pro laptop with a 15-inch screen! A normal person would have probably realized that the decisions they were making needed a change because something had gone seriously wrong.

See, I am not that normal person in any way, shape, or form as far as I am concerned. I am a master of destroying every single thing that I could love or care about. For example, I have to work from 4:00 p.m. until probably 12:00 or 1:00 in the morning tomorrow. Instead of sleeping, I am pounding out pages in my journal at 6:00 in the morning. Even when it comes to something as simple as this, I can't get my priorities to line up and make sense to another individual in the same way that they make sense to me. See, I would rather stay up all night for the sake of filling my journal than say, "I can write tomorrow after work."

All right, I have to take another time-out to explain the phone conversation I just had, as well as the importance. While I was sitting here writing, my aunt (Dad's sister) called and told me that she was gonna buy me a plane ticket back to North Carolina and wanted to know if I could leave today. Ha! If it were only that simple.

Friday afternoon, I actually called [and talked] her in to buying me a ticket to anywhere on the mainland because, and I quote, "I am stranded on this island and will never be able to get off of it." But all of this is a time-out that I'll focus on in greater detail in pages to come. And, before I go any further, I have left my house and I'm watching the sun come up over Waikiki beach. Seeing as how my days here are now limited, I seriously have the desire to take advantage of every single second I have remaining on this island.

I think I am going to spend my entire day sitting on the beach, watching the waves, surfers, tourists, and locals as they soak up another day on the island that saved my life.

So, where was I???? Ahhhhh . . . oh yeah!

Sitting in my car, locked out of the apartment my wife and I had shared in downtown Portland, Maine. See, the reason my wife wouldn't let me into the apartment is because I had been stealing money and lying and pretty much had refused to sober up long enough to give her the love she deserved.

At this point of the game, I had already thrown away 90 percent of my personal belongings and was getting ready for two days of sleeping in my car. I had spent all of my money and several thousand dollars of my wife's money on drugs, and my gas tank was almost empty.

I said my good-byes to my wife and took my computer to the pawn shop for one more high and gas money to anywhere outside of the state of Maine. I picked up one more shot of heroin and two or three good shots worth of cocaine, filled my gas tank, and hit the road. I don't remember exactly how much money I had, but I do know that I only had enough gas money to make it to Delaware. I pulled my car into a Western Union parking lot somewhere around two o'clock in the morning and climbed into my backseat to lay it down for the night.

When I woke up in the morning, I called my good friend in North Carolina and begged her to wire me some money! And being a true friend, she wired me $100 and told me to come directly to her house when I made it into town. I told her I would, hung up the phone, and proceeded to call my grandfather for an extra $100. Within an hour, I had $200 and was off for North Carolina—Charlotte, to be exact.

It was a good feeling to have $200 minus another tank of gas, Red Bull, and pack of smokes driving down the road. Then it hit me: *I'm about to start withdrawing from heroin at any moment now, and even if I drive straight to Charlotte, there's no way I'm gonna be able to work out a shot of heroin today.*

Afraid

Afraid of the pen.
Afraid of the paper.

The blank pages,
The empty journals,
The days that go by,
The lack of inspiration,
The lack of poems.

Afraid of failure.
Afraid of the downfall.

The dope sickness,
The cold jail cells,
The pain that passes by,
The lack of reality,
The lack of living.

Afraid of what they think.
Afraid of how they see me.

The lost days,
The missing father,
The ache that haunts me,
The lack of reliability,
The lack of loving.

Afraid of the asphalt.
Afraid of the beach.

The morning sunshine,
The empty organs,
The people passing by,
The lack of finances,
The lack of motivation.

Afraid of dying alone.

Envious!

Most people are envious of the rich or the famous or the people who are more attractive or have more toys.

Envious of others' cars, jobs, wives, college degrees, Louis Vuitton wallets, purses, steak dinners, musical talents, artistic talents, skills, athletic ability, laziness, lack of laziness—hell, the list could go on forever. I am not going to lie—I've been severely envious of all of this shit that's been listed so far. But right now, I'm envious of all of these crazy lunatic patients that are still getting handfuls of amazing medications. I'm really envious of all these patients who freak out and get shots of Thorazine or Haldol in the ass, then mellow out like the world is such a beautiful thing.

Damn it, I have to wait two-and-one-half hours until I can get my hands on my Valium and Ambien. Believe me when I say I'd kill someone for a Xanax right now. On top of all this anxiety, a Valium and Ambien won't even give me a head change. I am here to get sober, and all I think about is getting fucked up on some kind of pharmie.

I want to start flipping out over tables and throwing chairs so the staff will hold me down and give me a beautifully potent shot in the ass that will lay me down for the night. They would know I was faking the whole routine before I finished flipping the first table, though.

I'm envious! I'm a drug addict with no access to drugs. I'm envious of every social addict, social drinker, or asshole who can shoot heroin or cocaine once or twice a week, then put the needle or straw down for another three months.

Envious of all the crazy people locked in this psych ward that get new visitors every single day between 7:00 and 8:00 p.m. I don't have any friends on this godforsaken island—and I sure as hell don't have any family that wants anything to do with me. Fuck it. I'm envious of everything right now . . .

> people with cars,
> cash,
> freedom,
> girlfriends,
> nice clothes,
> lovers,
> friends,
> family,
> steaks,
> beach dates,
> good coffees,
> good sex,
> cereal,
> cigarettes,
> and
> shots of heroin.

Stuck in This Realm

I ask for a sword
and they treat me like
a madman.
When I speak of swords
I speak of the pen.
The pen is mightier
than the sword.

I love pens like
a madman
loses marbles.
It takes a sword for me
to complete my battles.

When unarmed I'm
quite useless.
When armed I
conquer pages with
Erato at my side.

If presented with the option
I would choose pen over
the sword any day of the week
because my pen speaks in volumes.
Sometimes in volumes even
I cannot understand,
sometimes to put it simply,
it's complicated.

They watch me as I write
at the bar,

as I smoke cigarettes,
and chug PBR.
I can see the question
in their eyes
as they wonder why I fill
these pages.

In all reality, I don't
even truly understand why
I feel the need to
fill these pages.
I just know I have to.

When it comes down to
it, it
doesn't even really
matter as long as the
pen continues running
across the pages—
my madness is put
to rest
and
the .38 sleeps
for another night.

I wander through these
pages like Christ
roamed through the desert
with no hope of becoming
complete—is irrelevant!

The only difference
is Christ learned a lesson
while I continue to struggle

and slowly make it through
this miserable existence.
I can't help but be
persistent
as I fumble through
life,
pages,
journals,
and
pens,
and still want more
as I attempt to be true.

But nothing ever happens
so I remain still.
Still as a ghost
as these thoughts
infect my spirit,
thoughts
and soul.

Forever lost and searching
for
the true meaning
of time and you
are absolutely no help
whatsoever.

So I remain stuck
in this realm and you
could care less
about my head
so you leave me
stranded.

Monkeys

The worst part of addiction is the misinterpretation that it can be conquered, or in a sense, forgotten about and reversed.

The reality of addiction is that it sits on your shoulder like some kind of demonic monkey that never stops chirping and consistently shoves the worst possible ideas into your head.

Now a normal person, for example, would punch the monkey in the face and go on living as if nothing had ever happened, which believe it or not, makes absolute sense. An addict, on the other hand, places serious thought and energy into every single word that fumbles out of that damn monkey's mouth. And, ten out of ten times believes every ounce of insanity that seems to be the only option available.

It turns into a never-ending battle that always results in rock bottoms and failure. Hell, addicts define insanity as "doing the same thing over and over again and expecting different results." *It never happens though. NEVER!*

Every time I put a needle into my arm, I am convinced that tomorrow I will not, and sometimes I don't. However, by the end of the week, I have put $600 worth of heroin and/or coke into my arm. And then I am off and running again.

Once I am off and running, there is not a single thing in this world that can stop me other than the police or a bullet to the head. And that is a scary fucking thought when it boils down to do it. It truly feels as though you have no control over your life whatsoever, and that's a painful reality that never diminishes or vanishes from a true addict's ever-so-helpless mentality.

So, we find ourselves in 12-Step meetings, detoxes, jails, prisons, and on the street pounding pavement, begging for change, and battling daily to keep those monkeys at bay. The depressing part is that the damn monkeys win 9.5 times out of 10, and we accept this pathetic existence and rarely give them a run for their money.

In the never-ending, infinite battle of sobriety, the monkeys are kicking our ass like the starting lineup of the nineties Chicago Bulls! The monkeys have Phil Jackson in their corner, and he just keeps stacking up championship rings.

It's time for the junkies to get someone strong in their corner . . . in our corner.

We need all the damn help we can get at this point—to hell with Phil Jackson, we need Buddha, Christ, Shiva, Erato, Apollo, each other, and an open mind on our team. Once we have a lineup like that, those damn monkeys don't have a chance!

Today

(Wilmington, North Carolina, 2010)

Life is like a massive puzzle, except you are only given one piece at a time. Each year you stumble across another piece and somehow manage to figure out how and where that piece fits into your overall character and life as a whole.

They say that change is the only constant, but I'm gonna have to disagree with that because a lot of my puzzle pieces have been constants. Despite all the change and all the ups and downs in my world, there have managed to be a handful of constants, and they're imbedded into my soul—things like Chuck Taylor shell toes, new plain white T-shirts, strong cups of coffee, the San Antonio Spurs, and Dodgers baseball.

My father was always a Dodgers fan. I can remember being a kid living in LA and my father taking me to Dodgers games. I remember going to batting practice to get baseball cards signed and eating Dodger dogs until I was sick to my stomach. I can remember moving to the East Coast, where everyone was wearing Yankee hats, Red Sox hats—and I almost fell into myself until I remembered my roots, my family, and that Dodger blue-and-white that I still wear on my head to this day.

Another one of those puzzle-piece constants is my love for literature and the art of writing. Everybody else in my family spent time drawing and painting, but it never managed to click with me like writing. They were good at it, I wasn't, but I found my niche of creativity in journals, blank pages, and painting pictures with words. That reminds me . . . I had an ex-girlfriend who was a photographer, and she would say, "A picture is worth a thousand words," and I would tell her, "Give me seventeen syllables and I'll paint a thousand pictures in your mind."

I was writing a lot of Haiku during that relationship and was learning very well the pains of the "business" of writing and the mailboxes full of submissions and rejections.

Now, this next constant may come across as an oxymoron, but I assure you it is not. A large part of my puzzle involves me moving to new cities, states, countries, apartments, houses, etc. I know moving a lot comes across as a "change" instead of a "constant," but in my life it is not. See, it's a constant for me to move every six months to a year, and that's just the way it is. I'll get into this constant in greater detail a little further down the road, because it's the next constant, the next puzzle piece, that carries the most weight.

Sixteen years, yup . . . for the last sixteen years of my life, my most consistent constant and defining characteristic has been addiction and the never-ending whirlpool battle of—even more specifically—heroin addiction.

So slowly but surely, this puzzle is coming together. This list of constants that fit together to paint a picture of the thirty-two years, thirty-two hard years of what I would like to call my life. I know I really haven't painted a Picasso, so to speak, but I have slapped together a little something to pick up on.

Another one of my constants is that I've always been skinny as hell and have never been able to break six feet in height. Standing up perfectly straight, I might reach 5' 11"—but for the record, I'll say 5' 10" and 155 pounds soaking wet.

So thus far, the painting should look something like this: a lanky character with a white T-shirt, Dodgers hat, and Chuck Taylors, wandering from city to city, shooting heroin, filling journals, and hanging out in coffee shops with some sort of literature nearby.

Now for the sake of better painting, I'd like to throw in that I have brown hair, brown eyes, and that I'm covered in tattoos. You wanna talk about constants . . . tattoos . . . permanent unless covered up. I am way past the removal stage. Tattoo removal is for drunken mistakes, small-scale tramp stamps, and Tasmanian devils on ankles. I, on the other hand, have entire limbs artistically stained with symbolic images that remind me of where I have been in life . . . but even more so, where I long to be.

That's important to understand! A lot of people regret tattoos, but I sure as hell don't. Even the shitty ones, the homemade tattoos, jailhouse tattoos done by some shady character with a sewing needle and bottle of India ink. I still remember my first tattoo like it was yesterday, the same way I remember my first joint, my first kiss, my first line of meth off a toilet seat in the girls' bathroom at Club Baja, and the same way I remember my first shot of heroin—not to be confused with the first time I snorted it . . . two totally different ballgames two years apart from one another.

So this thought brings me to my next objective in the pages to follow, their purpose, but even more so to ease the madness in my life that is set into motion the minute I put down the pen.

When a painter paints, he is not usually painting for you! He is painting because creativity has consequence. It is a madness that has to be released. Some release it with music, some with paint, and I release it with wide-ruled paper and preferably a pen with black ink.

First and foremost, I am writing this for me, for my sanity, while allowing you a window into my madness—a brief glimpse of a life lived differently from yours, a stream of stories, memories, and experiences that paint a picture of my world. Remember, they are all true, so if the smoking guns want to dig up my past like that dude that wrote *A Million Little Pieces*, then go for it.

I really feel for the poor guy. The guy writes a best seller and has it snatched out from underneath him because he wasn't Neal Cassady or Bukowski and was nothing more than a wannabe . . . unable to tell truth, caught up in the fantasy, poor guy. Hell, I used to idolize guys like Cassady, Hunter S., and Bukowski, mostly because I could identify with them—minus the fame, of course.

The other day, I was reading somewhere that Bukowski is the most copied writer of my time. More people try to copy his style than any other contemporary American writer. What a shame!

I mean, hell, don't get me wrong—I copied Bukowski's style for a few journals when I was in my early twenties, but I also copied Burroughs and the sporadic formats of Emily Dickinson. Copying and practicing a variety of styles can help ya pin down your own style and your own method of dealing with blank pages, but I'll be damned if I had the balls to copy Bukowski and submit it. That's like trying to be Michael Jackson, wearing one glove and doing the moonwalk and all the while telling people you got this new flavor—fresh on the scene.

Anyway, where was I? Maybe copying all those sporadic rhyme schemes and patterns caused me to become a sporadic thinker. I'm all over the place these days.

I guess I need to figure out how and where I'm gonna start this whole thing off. I could start with my parents, grandparents, my childhood, psychological evaluations as to what went wrong—or I could start with my full-blown addiction and work my way back to the womb. There's probably a million different ways that this madness could start up and all of which could take off in any variety of directions. The way my brain trails into tangents and irrelevant details, there really is no telling which way I will take off.

I guess for the sake of writing with thought and to avoid the overthinking of writer's block, I'll just start with today and let the tangents work their way through yet another blank page.

Today has been pretty simple so far. I didn't sleep hardly at all last night, but that's to be expected, seeing as how I'm still in my first week of heroin withdrawal. About five or six days ago, I checked myself into this locked detox facility here in Wilmington, NC, and actually managed to tough through the first couple of days of withdrawal without signing myself outta the place to rush and find my way to what my body was screaming for: another shot of heroin.

This wasn't my first trip to one of these types of facilities, but I swear to God I hope it's the last. These types of places treat ya like an animal, feed you slop, and take your shoelaces, belts, and anything else you could use to hang or hurt yourself with. I've never really been the suicidal type, but there have been a few occasions that I might have taken a belt or shoelace and choked the hell out of another patient or pill-stingy doctor!

I don't know about anyone else, but when I'm coming off of dope, I turn into an impatient, angry little man. For those of you who don't know, heroin withdrawal is not a stroll in the park, and although it is physically impossible to fall over and die from opiate detox, trust me when I say that death seems like a more reasonable alternative.

You know sayings like "dope sickness," "cold turkey," and "kicking the habit" all come from the misery of opiate withdrawal. "Dope sickness" is the physical and mental process that starts up its evil ways as the heroin is wearing off and exiting the system. The longer you have been doing the heroin, the worse the dope sickness.

For me, it starts with gagging over my morning coffee, and shortly after, the runny nose starts; the flu-like symptoms kick in and progressively get worse until I get that fabulous shot into my veins. And if that shot doesn't get into my veins, the pain becomes unbearable. All my joints and muscles begin to ache, and my legs become restless, jerking and kicking—hence the term "kicking the habit."

Then the hot and cold sweats start as the body covers itself with goose bumps, which is where the term "cold turkey" comes from. Oh, and this isn't it. Not even close. The vomiting and diarrhea kick in, making eating and sleeping a thing of the past as my body gets weaker and weaker, making me even more restless as each minute takes a lifetime to pass by.

This sickness can last up to a month, but usually by two or three days, you're willing to steal an old woman's purse to get a shot into your veins or put a bullet through your temple to get out of the misery that you know is only beginning.

I would love to explain heroin withdrawal in further detail, but I swear to God, just the thought of it gives me enough anxiety to lose my cool.

So, this leads me back to today . . . back to the past few days, back to the failure and depression and lingering misery that is weighing me down like an anchor. I had been doing well, had two decent kitchen jobs, was in good health—and heroin was one of the furthest things from my mind.

I slipped . . . thought I could do just one shot and leave it alone the next day and continue forward with my six months of progress. But that never happens. If that were the case, I wouldn't be an addict. I would just be a social heroin user, if there is even such a thing out there. People can drink socially or smoke herb or cigs socially, so I'm sure there are some assholes out there that use dope socially. The reason I call them "assholes" is because I'm jealous of them. I've never been able to use anything socially. If I drink, I drink to get drunk. I drink until I black out, vomit, get punched out by some champion twice my size, or end up in a jail cell.

So, to paint the picture of where I am right now goes a little something like this.

I had been clean for six months, rationalized shooting one simple bag of heroin, within a week was shooting 10 bags a day, and within a month lost both jobs, all my money, and almost lost my place to live. I drained $2,000 of my girlfriend's cash into my arms and began pawning anything that wasn't bolted down. That's addiction, my friend. What started as one shot led to a little over thirty days of absolute misery and destruction. I turned into a tornado, destroying anything in its path. Before signing myself into detox, I was begging strangers—or should I say, making up random stories of sympathy—to get cash to shake the sickness.

To make things even worse, if I had already managed a few shots of heroin in a particular day, I'd start shooting cocaine or smoking crack. I always enjoyed a good speedball as long as the downer side was stronger than the upper side of the concoction.

So yeah . . . I signed myself into a locked detox seconds before losing my girlfriend and minutes away from losing the roof over my head. I didn't have a dime in my pocket, was outta cigs, and had to have my girl drop me off at the detox because my car was out of gas and probably wouldn't have made it to the end of the block before shitting out.

The detox was cold and all lit up with fluorescent lights. They always are. They keep it cold to kill the germs and keep it all lit up because addicts can't be trusted in the dark. The beds are always stiff and covered with plastic. If you sleep with all your clothes on, the thin little blankets might keep you warm temporarily.

You never know what kind of characters you're likely to run into in those types of places, so it's usually a good idea to keep your guard up. If you have been in as many jails and institutions as I have, it almost seems like second nature. I know what to expect, I know how to deal with it, and I'm sure I wear it on my face like a pro as soon as I walk into these cold, lit-up hallways. I've spent large and random chunks of my life in state-funded facilities, and they're never fun. They have a magical way of helping you realize how fucked-up your life really has become . . . seeing how you're locked up behind steel doors with no shoelaces and are forced to sleep with a light on so the staff or guards can always keep an eye on you.

Each facility has its own little traits and characteristics, but the basic backbone is the same in all of 'em. The only way I can describe that backbone is like this: detox centers are a combination of hospitals and jails, and if that doesn't plant a seed, I don't know what to tell ya.

So yeah . . . five days ago, I was in one of those godforsaken places until I signed myself out A.M.A. (Against Medical Advice). I got through the worst of the withdrawals and made them open up the steel doors to let me out. The coffee in there was caffeine-free, and you couldn't smoke cigs, so I "lost it."

Not only was I miserable from withdrawals, but I couldn't enjoy my two legal vices. Fuck that.

When I signed myself out, I wasn't even 100 percent sure that I wasn't gonna find a way to track down some dope and get high. By the time I signed out, it was already really late at night, so I managed to convince myself that I'd just wait till the next morning, wait for my girl to go to work, then get higher than two kites in a windstorm once I had the house to myself.

That didn't happen. I actually got some sleep that night and woke up feeling like the worst of the dope sickness was behind me. I was sick and tired of being sick and tired, and instead of calling my dope-connect, I called some people I knew from Narcotics Anonymous. They told me not to use dope no matter what and if I was feeling squirrelly, I needed to get off my ass and get with some folks that were clean and sober.

To put it simply, I made the difficult decision of getting into my car and hitting up an NA meeting, and I actually spent the rest of the day and night hanging out with people that had been through what I was going through. They were slowly teaching me that life can actually be fun without getting high every day. Now, to the normal person, that comes across as quite an easy accomplishment, but when you've been getting high almost every day for sixteen years, life with drugs is an awkward and painful reality.

I would like to think that I put some substantial clean time together over the past sixteen or seventeen years, but I haven't. Alcohol, weed, benzos—I always had something to help me cope on a daily basis. Around the age of twenty-five, I got my act together and put down the needle and the dope, but I picked up the bottle. It was always something . . . I always needed another drink, another pill, another hit, and another lie to cover up my bullshit.

All that aside, I am clean today, and I haven't used any dope in going on a week. I don't know about tomorrow, but I haven't gotten high today.

Afterword

Micah returned twice in May 2014 – briefly on Mother's Day with a beautiful message of love and instruction to live in joy and later for six hours on what would have been his birthday, May 17th. The energy of the visit felt as though he simply wanted to 'hang out' with me, affirming the healing power of the spirit releasement work we did six months earlier.

Through the experiences with my son during life and since his death, concerns about working in the "invisible" space have disappeared. For someone who spent her career as an international financial executive, it has taken courage and fortitude to bring this spiritual awareness to others.

I have surrendered to God's Will and have asked for help to bring an awareness to healing addiction, especially to the inner peace that is possible through greater understanding of why the addiction is present in the first place. I have learned that some can be healed in this lifetime on this physical plane, while others cannot. Each case is unique.

God has blessed me with the gift and ability to communicate with beings that are not visible to the naked eye. I feel the vibrational differences of their diversity and sometimes even a sense of their personality. Some are very matter-of-fact, but *always* in a benevolent manner.

I also have the gift of communication with those who are dying, nonresponsive, or in a coma. I am able to communicate with their guides and sometimes loved ones who have already crossed over.

I can assist during the death process to whatever extent God allows. For example, sometimes I receive communication for the family. Sometimes the individual's guides contact me to help the individual, who may be in fear or another uncomfortable in-between state. The guides tell me what to do to help, especially if the individual knew me in the physical.

I do not do anything for them; I guide them from the physical plane. If anything confusing for them shows up, I often can assist in bringing clarity to them—which brings greater ease and comfort in their transition.

God has graced and blessed me with these gifts through the pain and suffering I experienced having a child with severe addiction—trying everything I could to help him but being powerless to change anything. God has given me the courage to push the edge, exploring unknown territories to find healing. I am grateful beyond measure and am available to share what I know with those who seek change and healing in their lives.

Just as we are born at the perfect moment for our energy to enter this Earth, there is a perfect moment for us to leave this Earth. We are complete.
~Rinpoche

About the Author

Mindy Miralia is a pioneer and adventurer, catalyst and change agent. Often referred to as an "edge runner," she believes strongly in getting in front of opportunities to pave the way for the future. She is passionate about helping people find meaning in life, relieving unnecessary pain and suffering, and holding the space to help individuals make shifts in their lives that bring inner peace and personal transformation.

Mindy holds a BS in biology from the University of Houston and an MBA in finance from the University of Colorado. She holds certification from the National Institute for the Clinical Application of Behavioral Medicine in Navigating the Soul's Journey, is a certified Spiritual Counselor and is also certified in numerous healing systems, including Reiki, ThetaHealing, and Reconnective Healing. Mindy travels the globe working with indigenous peoples to learn and deepen her abilities.

Mindy's lifelong extra sensory and mediumistic abilities helped her develop the transformational healing work she facilitates today. She is a facilitator who helps clients find a greater understanding of the human workings of mind, thought, and consciousness to support improved life experiences. Mindy works with individuals and groups by phone and in person, and travels frequently. She lives in Charlotte with her husband, Rock, and their dog, Harmony—a frequent hospice visitor as part of Mindy's work with Hospice & Palliative Care Pet Therapy.

For more information please visit www.mindymiralia.com and www.TheHeroInHeroin.com

CPSIA information can be obtained at www.ICGtesting.com
Printed in the USA
LVOW10s0927100415

433955LV00001B/8/P